PATTERNS OF THOUGHT IN RIMBAUD AND MALLARMÉ

FRENCH FORUM MONOGRAPHS

63

Editors R.C. LA CHARITÉ and V.A. LA CHARITÉ

For complete listing, see page 135

Patterns of Thought in Rimbaud and Mallarmé

JOHN PORTER HOUSTON

FRENCH FORUM, PUBLISHERS
LEXINGTON, KENTUCKY

The volumes in this series are printed on acid-free,
long-life paper and meet the requirements of the
American National Standard for Permanence of Paper
for Printed Materials
Z 39.48-1984.

Library of Congress Catalog Card Number 85-80741

ISBN 0-917058-64-X

Printed in the United States of America

TABLE OF CONTENTS

FOREWORD

My first book, published some twenty years ago, dealt with Rimbaud and attempted above all the elucidation of difficult poems and passages of poems with the analytic tools at my disposal.[1] Its reception was, on the whole, favorable, and the work continues, apparently, to be regarded as sound. The present book is rather different in that I have tried to place Rimbaud and Mallarmé within a much larger framework of ideas than a young scholar usually is capable of drawing on. The stylistic matters which preoccupied me then and more recently are scarcely touched on here.[2] I decided, after various attempts, that, in dealing with Rimbaud's and Mallarmé's most complex work, it is almost impossible to join, in readable fashion, thorough-going explication of verbal detail with the exposition of their larger intellectual designs as they extend throughout their respective œuvres.

The notion of intellectual design, however, needs some explanation. I have entitled this book "patterns of thought" rather than something like "Rimbaud's thought" or "Mallarmé's themes" because I wished to distinguish in their work an order of thought which transcends any collection of opinions or aphoristic affirmations one might find there. Nor am I talking about themes in the sense that Rimbaud uses the "theme" of wandering or Mallarmé the "theme" of women's hair: Jean-Pierre Giusto's *Rimbaud créateur* (Paris: Presses Universitaires de France, 1980) exemplifies at great length this approach. However, one could list themes and collect isolated statements in abundance without ever coming to what I regard as the serious intellectual core of their work—for, as it will be obvious, I consider Rimbaud and Mallarmé both to be poets of high intellect, despite their respective reputations for intoxication and preciosity. The patterns of thought I investigate determine the entire shape of poems and are on the order of tripartition in schemes of history, distinctions between the transcendent and the immanent, cyclical ordering, and the escape from dualistic philosophical stances. These are not abstractions of the same kind as Rimbaud's theme of flowers or Mallarmé's remarks on Wagner, although such details may well be subsumed under the larger intellectual design. We are dealing with forms of thought, much like esthetic forms, which can be filled with varying specific concepts.

In order better to seize on the principal thought patterns in Rimbaud and Mallarmé, I have made a number of comparisons with writers who, for one reason or another, seem to illuminate the work of the two French poets. Most of these writers predate Rimbaud and Mallarmé; I often stress the background against which the latter two wrote rather than their prophetic modernism. The exclusive emphasis on Rimbaud's and Mallarmé's relation to 20th-century literature produces a distortion for which I have tried to compensate. However, the study of the 19th-century background does not in every case indicate a more or less traceable influence. I am concerned, for example, with certain characteristics of Romantic theology, both technical and poetic: what we can learn from Schleiermacher or Blake seems to me valuable in establishing a perspective on Rimbaud. With Mallarmé, on the other hand, we can perceive the actual influence, however indirect, of Hegel, though Mallarmé interpreted Hegel in a highly personal fashion. Furthermore, there are many aspects of Hegelian thought which clarify Mallarmé's cast of mind despite the fact that he was possibly unacquainted with them. I fully explore the parallels between Hegel and Mallarmé not so much to prove an extensive influence as to illuminate Mallarmé's often elliptic ways of thinking.

I am not altogether certain that the patterns of thought I distinguish are comparable to the convictions which guide many people—both the gifted and the foolish—in their practical life, or that what I have found is intellectual biography in the same sense in which a major philosopher may be said to have one. James Joyce once said, when pressed for the importance of Vico's cyclical historiography for his own work, "I would not pay overmuch attention to these theories, beyond using them for all they are worth."[3] I have tried to use such distinctions as I make for all they are worth without being under any illusion about the everyday significance they might have for the poet. The patterns of thought I am concerned with may have served the poet only in the ordering of his work and consequently constituted biographical material in a merely limited way.

My greatest hope for this book is that it will reveal Rimbaud and Mallarmé as poets of serious intelligence in the framework of 19th-century thought. Much of the latter, to be sure, may appear as folly to a logical positivist or anyone approaching that position; however, we must, if we are to read Rimbaud and Mallarmé, provisionally grant the vitality of Romantic theology or German dialectics. When we do so, some of Rimbaud and Mallarmé's uniqueness will vanish, but, on the other hand, so will the eccentricity that often seems to becloud their achievement.

I have translated nearly all lengthy or difficult quotations in verse or prose. Indeed, most prose other than that of *Une Saison en enfer* and the

Illuminations is given only in English because translation is often in itself one of the most succinct methods of interpretation and commentary. The necessity for quoting Rimbaud's poetic prose in French, the fact that he wrote little of an expository nature, and the slimness of Mallarmé's production of major verse have resulted in a far greater number of pages being devoted to Rimbaud than to Mallarmé. This disproportion does not reflect any disparity in their intellectual gifts or poetic worth, but has arisen out of the nature of the material. Nothing seems to me more sterile than the artificial antithesis between Rimbaud and Mallarmé created for the needs of hagiography or classroom exposition. In the following pages there will be found no attempt at a subtle, definitive ranking of Mallarmé and Rimbaud between themselves or in a larger scale of poetic values. Their greatness is indisputable, as is witnessed by the large number of serious and intelligent works of explication devoted to their poetry. I am concerned with elucidating how such poetry could come about in the context of contemporary and earlier thought. My own explications are, therefore, sometimes one-sided and quite consciously corrective of other perfectly valid kinds of commentary. I offer them as an attempt to fill in the puzzling gap which has always seemed to exist between the achievement of Rimbaud and Mallarmé and previous literature. Psychological and biographical criticism, as well as purely structural analyses, have been carried very far in regard to both poets, but it seems to me that something remains to be said about their thought as recurrent patterns or even as informal systems.

Chapter I

RIMBAUD IN 1871

Almost all of Rimbaud's poetry from the first pieces preserved onward shows distinctive features, but it is hard to find a common ground between, for example, the anti-war poems of the summer of 1870 and the Wanderlust pieces of October of the same year. Perhaps the notion that an evil society is opposed to nature and freedom most generally underlies Rimbaud's imagery; it is a common Romantic attitude, suitable to a somewhat alienated adolescent, which was perhaps more an assumption on Rimbaud's part than a conscious theme. Indeed, if we are looking for a consciously distinctive feature of his poems, we may find it most perhaps in the *self-*consciousness of his poetic activity.[1] However, the totality of Rimbaud's experience from summer 1870 through the spring of 1871 had a retrospective significance independent of Rimbaud's varied and passing poetic concerns.[2] This first great period in his development as an artist coincided with a series of historical events to which it has a relation well beyond the obvious ones. Shortly after the beginning of the Franco-Prussian War, the Emperor was captured, which satisfied the growing anti-imperial feeling in liberal quarters, and the republic was declared, with some apprehensions, on the part of conservative politicians, of a popular uprising, as in 1848. The war seemed, from Rimbaud's native Charleville in the east, to threaten the bourgeoisie in particular, and finally the Commune was formed in Paris on March 17, 1871, a popular government which was depicted by the official government of France (in Versailles) as a red apocalypse in which all institutions were being destroyed.

It is likely that Rimbaud believed the propaganda released against the Commune, but his reaction was to sympathize with the revolutionary government. The insurrection represented for him the embodiment of Romantic political prophecies and theories, which he seems to have looked into during the winter of 1870-1871. The inevitable comparison which the public saw between the Commune and the Revolution of 1848 came to have an even greater relevance than it seemed to at first, for the Commune was violently suppressed during the *semaine sanglante* (May 21-28, 1871), an action comparable to the repressive measures taken by the army in June 1848. And so a cycle was terminated, which had begun with republican and extreme leftist agitation on the eve of the Franco-Prussian War. The cycle of aspiration and disillusionment, dejection, or defeat first presented itself to Rimbaud's mind as the rhythm of history, and it was to be integrated into his imaginative patterns, as it corresponded to one aspect of his sensibility. This is the kind of relation of sociological experience to poetic creation which is usually obscured by masses of anecdotal material.

Before the repression of the Commune, however, perhaps after a trip to Paris during it, Rimbaud wrote his two most important pieces of non-artistic prose, the letters of May 13 to his former teacher Georges Izambard and of May 15 to Paul Demeny, a poet he was modestly acquainted with. The sense of apocalyptic change is strong in both of these *lettres du voyant*, a *voyant* being, in Romantic social theory, a leader of people as well as a seer. Perhaps because he could hardly hope for any real understanding on the part of his correspondents, Rimbaud did not attempt to make his ideas seem completely sequential and coherent. As it turned out, they actually represented a number of thoughts coexisting in his mind, which he was to exploit at different times and in different ways in the course of his poetic career. The important point must be made here that, having an unusual degree of education (far superior to that of most 19th-century French poets), high intelligence, and great enthusiasm for ideas, Rimbaud did not always think one notion at a time, write in only one style at a time, or conceive of life in only one way at a time; his mind was a rich storehouse of ideas and esthetic conceptions, which he drew on as circumstances moved him. It is a great mistake to imagine Rimbaud's work as either unvaryingly uniform or else proceeding too neatly from one notion to another, as if life were the Collège de Charleville and poetry an endless exercise in *dissertation française*. An excessively disjunctive view of his work, however, is perhaps less misleading than one of those synchronic interpretations which ignore all differences between texts.

In the juxtaposition of ideas which make up the *lettres du voyant*, Rimbaud speaks, with regard to progress, of a materialist future and, at the same time, of a universal intelligence or soul which seems to be related to that future. These apparently contradictory notions have something in common, however. "Materialist" is almost a code word for "anti-Catholic," with reference to the 18th-century French materialists, such as d'Holbach or La Mettrie. Moreover, the Church was endlessly charged in Romantic thought with neglecting the body and its needs. "Universal soul" is likewise a religiously subversive term, for it designates an impersonal reserve of power utterly different from the Christian God, whom Rimbaud saw, like a number of Romantics, as an evil old man in a remote heaven. Either, we should note, this universal spirit or oversoul, to use Emerson's ingenious term, may be represented as immanent, which leads to the notion that some Romantic poetry is pantheistic, or else there may seem to be a gap between ordinary experience and the world soul, in which case we are in the presence of a dualistic view of the universe comparable to the dualisms of Christianity. Rimbaud's world spirit, as it emerges from his vocabulary, is otherworldly, his thought dualistic, which is stressed by his referring to spirit as "the plenitude of the great dream," which is not our everyday state, and by his account of the poet's quest into the unknown reaches of the world soul *là-bas*, from which he brings back his strange discoveries. *Là-bas*, "down there," is an interesting term, contrasting with the *là-haut* of the traditional realm of God and suggesting an under-consciousness, or unconsciousness. This dualism of spirit and ordinary life, so different from the Wordsworthian notion of divine imagination as infused in our world, will have great consequences for Rimbaud's poetic thought as it evolves.

Upon this dualism is superimposed another one, which is that of revolutionary thought. For the proponent of revolution, the present is divided between the forces of reaction and his own impulsion forward. Thus, revolutionaries can forget, in the violence of their polemics, the ultimate utopian goal of a unified society towards which they theoretically tend. Some of Rimbaud's revolutionary poems, such as "Le Juste" or "Les Mains de Jeanne-Marie," seem consequently more Manichean than utopian-minded. Some revolutionary thinking also follows a para-Christian mythological scheme of original unity, subsequent division, and a return to oneness. In the second *lettre du voyant*, Rimbaud's sketch of the history of poetry shows this pattern, with its decline from the unity of art and action in ancient Greece and the ultimate recapturing, in a yet higher form, of poetry identified with power, after the long intervening centuries of games of versification. This scheme of history runs contrary to myths of defeat, and it is essential to observe the interplay of the two in Rimbaud's imagination.

Another important idea in the *lettres du voyant* is that the poet, in the course of his "deranging his senses," of which I shall speak later, becomes the great Accursed and the supreme Savant or repository of *science*. The terminology is derived from the primordial Biblical myth and was much exploited by Michelet and other unorthodox Romantic writers: he who is accursed is actually blessed, for he possesses the knowledge which Satan traditionally held and which God denied man (as in Baudelaire's "Litanies de Satan"). *Science*, in the older sense of knowledge, is a key term in Rimbaud's poetry. The tree of knowledge is that of *science* in French, and so the word has very rich connotations. The linguistic root would have also suggested, to someone of Rimbaud's education, the "ye shall be as gods": "eritis sicut dei *scientes* bonum et malum." All this reference to the accursed and to knowledge has, of course, nothing whatsoever to do with the demonology Huysmans and others dabbled in at the end of the century: Rimbaud's vocabulary stems from the mainstream of French Romantic thought and represents still another important source of dualistic thinking.

The curious thing about the *lettres du voyant*—one that has made them difficult to use for the interpretation of Rimbaud's verse—is that the poems written about that time do not seem to reflect the letters except for a general kind of revolutionary violence. The idea of the universal soul emerges more clearly in poems written a year later, and the word *science* does not become prominent in Rimbaud's work until the same time. It would seem that the purely conceptual side of the two letters needed to incubate before it took on poetic embodiment. It is clear that the two kinds of poems Rimbaud was writing as the Commune ended derive from other concerns than those voiced in the letters. There are fine ideological narratives, "Les Premières Communions" and "Les Poètes de sept ans," but the first is an elaborate development of Rimbaud's previous anti-Christian sentiments, and the second contains a vision of freedom and mankind redeemed which does not correspond especially to what Rimbaud has to say about the seer. There are also the very obscure "Le Cœur volé" and "Mes Petites Amoureuses"; a punning satire, "Chant de guerre parisien"; and a poem about the use of a chamberpot ("Accroupissements"), which might be called a satire in a loose sense. I am not concerned here with explicating any of these poems, but rather with tracing the theoretical basis of style which led Rimbaud to write such lines as the following, for which a translation would scarcely be feasible:

> Un hydrolat lacrymal lave
>   Les cieux vert-chou:
> Sous l'arbre tendronnier qui bave,
>   Vos caoutchoucs
> Blancs de lunes particulières
>   Aux pialats ronds
>
>   .   .   .   .
>
>   ("Mes Petites Amoureuses")

I do not think that this is by any means the language of the seer embodying a vision brought back from "down there." On the contrary, the subject matter consists of a satirical revulsion from ordinary girls as they appeared to Rimbaud at the time, and the diction is more contrived than visionary. This side of Rimbaud's inspiration, these lines laden with rare words, has its roots rather in the vituperative tradition. At the same time, we can distinguish some connection between satire and vision in the work of Hugo and in at least one poem of Rimbaud's from the spring of 1871.

Although there was much that was revolutionary and visionary in a general sense in French Romantic poetry, only Victor Hugo—and that rather late in his career—actually formulated a notion of language as parallel to or subsuming revolutionary action. He would perhaps not have done so, had it not been for his exile and the inspiration of his long *Châtiments* (1853), a satiric, prophetic, and apocalyptic work directed against Louis-Napoleon and the Second Empire. The analogy with Biblical prophecy was present in his mind, and the book is ideologically creative in that it moves from alienation to the vision of a new society. In actual verbal techniques, the volume is distinctly more audacious than Hugo's previous verse. In the highly rhetorical world of French politics since the Revolution, words at times functioned effectively as actions, and, in a sense, this work, popular in France in smuggled copies, added to the republican sentiment which did shape events: there was never another monarchy or empire in France after Louis-Napoleon. But it was later than *Châtiments* that Hugo thought the question of words and deeds through: in *Les Contemplations* (1856), the theme of the Word or logos plays an essential role. In a well-known pair of poems ("Réponse à un acte d'accusation" and its "Suite"), Hugo compares, with suitable stylistic examples, his effect on the French language with that of the Revolution on society. In the devious movement of these poems, he finally concludes, "Et le mot, c'est le Verbe, et le Verbe, c'est Dieu." Readers have tended to take this equation of word with logos and God as a far-fetched apothegm, but careful study of *Les Contemplations* shows how widely the theme is diffused and how Hugo establishes, quite incontrovertibly, that Christ's words, among others, have been forces comparable to material ones. Indeed, taking the logos in the sense of poetry, it is perfectly clear why Rimbaud wrote in the second *lettre du voyant*: "La poésie ne rythmera plus l'action"—poetry will bring about material actions. Rimbaud was also a Bible reader like Hugo and familiar with the reverence and power accorded words in both Testaments.[3]

We must look a bit closer, however, at the movement from the satiric word to the creative word, exemplified first in Hugo's progression from *Châtiments* to *Les Contemplations* and then in Rimbaud's extraordinary burst of poetic activity in the spring and summer of 1871. It is noticeable in both Hugo and Rimbaud, as well as in the Biblical prophets, that invective seems to release a great deal of verbal invention. Invective produces a certain illusion of power over its object, a power which seems generated by the rich detail of vituperation. The variety and inventiveness of the words involved can lead into a more creative kind of discourse as well—"toute parole étant idée," according to the second *lettre du voyant*. This passage from negative to positive invention occurs in various poems in Hugo's *Châtiments*, and Rimbaud, in one satiric poem, "Ce qu'on dit au poète à propos de fleurs," passes from a satire on outmoded Parnassian poetry to creations not unlike what the *bateau ivre* will encounter:

> Trouve, aux prés fous, où sur le Bleu
> Tremble l'argent des pubescences,
> Des calices pleins d'œufs de feu
> Qui cuisent parmi les essences!

(Seek out in mad meadows, where silvery pubescents tremble against the blue sky, flowers full of fire, eggs cooking amidst essences!)

The imperative verb would seem to correspond to the "trouver une langue" of the second *lettre du voyant*, although the imagery is scarcely so metaphysically inventive as is that of the poems of 1872. Rather, there are social and technological implications here. This is not quite yet the poetry of the Word, as we shall encounter it later. At the same time, we sense that a certain tendency towards seeing poetry as a creative logos is already present in "Ce qu'on dit au poète." The background to it lay in the rhetorical orientation of Rimbaud's schooling, in his thorough religious instruction (compulsory in all schools under the Second Empire), and in the philosophical coloring of much French Romantic social and historical thought, with its vast concepts not unlike those of Christianity and often parallel to them. It is noteworthy that the secular or religiously neutral idea of the imagination, so highly developed in the English world of fragmented, tepid, or conventional Protestantism, scarcely touched 19th-century French poets, whose thinking tended to be formed initially by reaction to highly dogmatic Catholicism, to which they opposed concepts of a theological nature.[4] Even more remote from the intellectual world Rimbaud grew up in are the empirical, nominalist tendencies of thought in the modern English-speaking countries. For example, the color of the vowels, which Hugo and Mallarmé thought about as well as Rimbaud, is part of a long tradition of identifying words and things, of seeing abstractions as concrete entities, and, in general, of involving oneself in the problems of the old pre-Kantian metaphysics, where questions of essences and absolute being are treated.[5]

Although "Ce qu'on dit au poète" does not represent Rimbaud's greatest attempt to bring back visions from "down there," it is important to see the revolutionary nature of the poem in a limited context. One singular aspect of the second *lettre du voyant* is the list of recent poets, the so-called Parnassians, whom Rimbaud praises. The very rapid development of his esthetic—including such different poems as "Mes Petites Amoureuses" and "Les Poètes de sept ans"—had completely outstripped the poetic conceptions of any contemporary (save Mallarmé), and yet Rimbaud was transfixed by the idea of living in Paris and participating in the literary world. (A bit later, Tristan Corbière, when living in Paris, apparently had the prudence never to go near another French poet.) The fundamental paradox of the artist who needs an audience and can find none equipped to understand his work was coming into Rimbaud's consciousness—his situation scarcely had any real parallels—and gave rise to the strange letter he sent Théodore de Banville in August 1871 and signed "Hercules slobbered," though identifying himself as the boy who had sent Banville a mythological poem the year before.

This time Rimbaud enclosed in his letter a copy of "Ce qu'on dit au poète," which parodies the styles of the Parnassians and concludes with a kind of brief poetic manifesto which is, to say the least, anti-Parnassian. The whole piece is based on the idea of plants: on the one hand, the plants of the real world ("les tabacs, les cotonniers!") and, on the other, those of the imaginary realm. The two categories of plants are either too undignified for the Parnassians or too rare for their slight imaginations to discover: "Des fleurs presque pierres, fameuses!— / Qui vers leurs durs ovaires blonds / Aient des amygdales gemmeuses!" This aggressively modernist esthetic, anticipating the ideas of Apollinaire's time, was probably suggested in part by the Saint-Simonians' praise of industry and productiveness, a notion we find later in Rimbaud, but the key to the poem is undoubtedly the absence of the word Beauty, preferably with a capital. The minor poets of the day tended towards a rather flaccid estheticism—a successful metaphor is a rare find in their work—and a pseudo-aristocratic love of Beauty. Rimbaud's avoidance of the term in an ars poetica, however brief, is significant: from an early stage on, he had conceived of poetry more in satiric and ideological terms than in purely esthetic ones. Later, epitomizing in *Une Saison en enfer* the beginnings of his divergence from the literary world and from society in general, he was to say, "Un soir, j'ai assis la Beauté sur mes genoux. —Et je la trouvai amère. —Et je l'ai injuriée." The Beauty he insulted is the "derisory" conception of it found in Parnassian poets.

Nevertheless, Rimbaud lived out the paradox of having outworn the Parnassian esthetic and yet of longing to occupy a place in the world of letters. He is said to have written "Le Bateau ivre" to show to poets in Paris as an example of his work, and certain aspects of the poem incline one to believe that he conceived of it as a sort of modified Parnassian poem, something very much of his own, yet which would nevertheless suggest the ideals of color, descriptiveness, and relative impersonality which Leconte de Lisle counseled to those who would listen. The more bizarre effects of vocabulary are gone, at the suggestion, by letter, of Verlaine, according to the traditional account of their first correspondence.[6] It seems unquestionable, moreover, that Rimbaud chose deliberately to echo, yet to differ greatly from, Léon Dierx's "Le Vieux Solitaire" (1864), which had been reprinted in the second series of Le Parnasse Contemporain (1869-1871) and which begins, "Je suis tel qu'un ponton sans vergues et sans mâts, / Aventureux débris des trombes tropicales." It is improper to say that Dierx's poem is a "source" of "Le Bateau ivre" in the usual sense of some darkly concealed object of pillage; everyone had read it, and Rimbaud wished to make his mark by using ostensibly the same material.

Early commentators were fond of exclaiming with wonder over Rimbaud's having written "Le Bateau ivre" without ever having seen the sea, and the observation seems to have become a pedagogical staple. The very absurdity of the remark, however, reveals something quite important about many readers' assumptions and why Rimbaud is often made out to be difficult in other ways than he really is. The notion that a writer seeks "experiences," which then provide him with his subject matter, lies behind this confusion over Rimbaud's inner and outer life. In 20th-century America, for example, the press so publicized Ernest Hemingway's quest for experience (pursued, ironically, in the face of declining literary powers) that the veriest philistine learned a writer must value experience above all. In France, the cult of experience owes more to Gide in its beginnings, but the results are the same. It is interesting to contrast Hemingway's (or Jack Kerouac's) quest for experience with the working methods of the 19th-century French Realists: Flaubert and Zola did research when they needed material for their novels, and it was a fairly orderly, rather academic activity that they imposed upon themselves. The modern notion of experience with its particular colorings—sensational, brutal, illicit, or otherwise—simply did not exist in the same form in Rimbaud's day, for it is an idea almost inseparable from the first-person or even third-person mode of fiction which closely follows the movements of consciousness and sensations within a realistic framework. The 19th-century literature of travel and exploration, which seems reflected at times in Rimbaud's work, shows a great curiosity about unusual sights and the relics of the past, but there is a qualitative difference between adventure of the older sort and the sense of experience conveyed in modern fiction. For a writer of some philosophical culture, however, experience can lie as well in ideas and language. One can even maintain that, with Rimbaud's creative view of language, the poem itself is the experience, the writing and reading of it an epistemological act. Modern ideas of experience, with their implication of a facile subsequent literary mimesis, show the shallow contempt for language which empiricism engenders.

It is important to insist on the nature of Rimbaud's language, for the matter of "Le Bateau ivre" risks being misunderstood, by virtue of a certain degree of Parnassian coloring and smoothness, for a simple extended comparison, such as we find in Dierx's "Le Vieux Solitaire," where the stages of man's life and of the boat's journey are neatly coordinated. Thus, we must refrain from a kind of allegorizing which would make of "Le Bateau ivre" a poem fashioned after the basically straightforward rhetoric of Leconte de Lisle and his followers.

"Le Bateau ivre" does indeed show, for the most part, the concern for composition, for the clear relations of parts to the whole, that we find in a carefully written Parnassian poem like Leconte de Lisle's "Sacra fames." The opening stanzas subtly convey the idea of revolt and the association of the boat with childhood. Verbs are much more dynamic than in most contemporary poetry and lead to the clearly set off description of the height of the boat's experience, which is called "le Poème de la Mer," a term congruent with Parnassian estheticism. The imagery, however, in its cosmological vastness, suggests communion with the universal soul or spirit; a mention of love implies the idea of the cycle of life. We initially at least take the boat and sea as conventional symbols of man and life. The grammatical-rhetorical structure is at once grand and traditionally elegant, with its turning point in the conditional perfect tense ("J'aurais voulu"), situating the voyage in the more distant past and in the long, repeated, suspensive construction *moi qui.* So much clarity and descriptive brilliance may, however, lull our sense of the detail in the last four stanzas, which, curiously, constitute something like four possible endings for the poem.

First the weary boat contemplates the night and thinks of the "future Vigor" and thousands of golden birds concealed in the dark:

> J'ai vu des archipels sidéraux! et des îles
> Dont les cieux délirants sont ouverts au vogueur:
> —Est-ce en ces nuits sans fond que tu dors et t'exiles,
> Million d'oiseaux d'or, ô future Vigueur?—

(I have seen archipelagos of stars! and islands whose ecstatic skies are open to the sea-wanderers: "Is it in these limitless nights that you sleep and retire, O future Vigor, O you thousands of golden birds?")

This imagery is revolutionary and apocalyptic, as "vigor" implies the rise of the oppressed, with gold symbolizing a golden age and birds a soaring redemptive movement. Some vast dawn is hinted at, in which life will be transformed by man's new power.

The stanza which follows, on the other hand, dwells on the natural cycle of physical decay and is appropriate to an allegory of the stages of life. "Acrid love" has worn the boat out, in keeping with the negative connotations of heterosexuality at this stage in Rimbaud's poetry (cf. "Les Sœurs de charité"):

> Mais, vrai, j'ai trop pleuré! Les Aubes sont navrantes.
> Toute lune est atroce et tout soleil amer:
> L'âcre amour m'a gonflé de torpeurs enivrantes.
> O que ma quille éclate! O que j'aille à la mer!

(But, truly, I have wept too much. The dawns are heartbreaking. Any moon is horrible and any sun bitter. Acrid love has filled me with intoxicating torpors. Let me go to the sea! Let my keel burst and let me dissolve there!)

Here the wretched dawn contrasts specifically with the anticipated one of the preceding stanza. The boat-man desires death. (The difficulty of the last line is simply the use of hysteron proteron, or reversal of time sequence, a familiar figure of Latin poetry which Rimbaud had absorbed in his classical studies.) Disillusionment becomes the rhythm of man's life, a rhythm which is also that of history, as Rimbaud knew it in 1870-1871.

The penultimate stanza of "Le Bateau ivre," about a child sailing his toy boat in a puddle, concerns not a boat which has retreated to the coastline, as just previously, but a land-locked plaything:

> Si je désire une eau d'Europe, c'est la flache
> Noire et froide où vers le crépuscule embaumé
> Un enfant accroupi plein de tristesses, lâche
> Un bateau frêle comme un papillon de mai.

(If I want European water, it is the cold, black puddle where, in the sweet-scented twilight, a squatting child full of melancholy sets off a boat fragile as a May butterfly.)

Here we can read the poem as private fantasy, a child's intuition and verbal creation. The stanza is interestingly ambiguous in associations: on the one hand, May suggests the waxing year; on the other, the dark, cold water seems to hint at the important cyclical theme that the exercise of the creative word ends in a bleak sense of being cast back into a profane, dead world.

The presence of more than one conceivable ending for "Le Bateau ivre" has a curious analogy with the movement of "Les Poètes de sept ans" and shows something fundamental about Rimbaud's imagination that we shall encounter again later. The boy poet in the earlier poem has a rather hostile and incomplete heterosexual experience, but turns immediately to telling of something more satisfying. Balancing his hatred of God, whom he reads about in the Bible, is a dream of young golden crowds soaring in light and scent: the social apocalypse is a triumph over the evil orthodox God, a creature of wan December Sundays. However, the climax of the child's imaginative life is not this dream of a collectivity, which might seem to be a definitive fulfillment of his aspirations, but rather an individual fantasy in which his room metamorphoses into a ship, as he makes up his novel (his own literature is experience for the poet) about seas, storms, and skies, the cosmological vision. The boy's dreams are only in part about the regeneration of mankind, which explains why Rimbaud is a less consistently or orthodoxly revolutionary poet than the second *lettre du voyant* might suggest.

To return to the end of "Le Bateau ivre," Rimbaud obviates any one reading of the poem as exclusive and definitive by concluding with a stanza that reminds one of the old principle that allegory should have a coherent literal meaning:

> Je ne puis plus, baigné de vos langueurs, ô lames,
> Enlever leur sillage aux porteurs de cotons,
> Ni traverser l'orgueil des drapeaux et des flammes,
> Ni nager sous les yeux horribles des pontons.

(I can no longer, bathed in your languor, O waves, follow close on the cotton boats, or pass haughty flags and spurting flames, or swim under the terrible eyes of the prisonships.)

The last lines deal with nothing but a decaying boat, a boat which is not obviously a child or man or dream. The imagery of proud boats, which insists on the literal level of the poem, appears to be a condensation of poems in Hugo's *Les Orientales* about the many gorgeous flags ships bear and about the fireboats once used in naval combats.

One could schematize the last four stanzas of "Le Bateau ivre" as dealing in sequence with the social-apocalyptic, sexual life, verbal creation, and the decay of all matter, but the important common element of the last three is cyclic decline. It is curious that we can find a hint of this pattern as early as "Ophélie" (spring 1870), an unconventional picture of a symbolic Ophelia floating for thousands of years on the waters, after being overcome by "winds of bitter freedom" and by the voices of nature, love, and the sea. Ideological aspirations are countered by the downward movement of matter seeking rest in insentience.

This negative cycle pattern, which we have now seen in history and poetry, epitomizes also Rimbaud's longings for Paris and his unfortunate encounter with and separation from the "artisticaillerie," as he called them, the beauty-minded and conservative men of letters, who quite justly found Rimbaud's manners atrocious. Rimbaud, for his part, discovered what

Proust was later to insist on so much: authors and their works are different things. Poetry no longer existed as disembodied texts in books, as in the Charleville days, but was incarnated in vain, frivolous men. A point of view other than Rimbaud's confirms this; Mallarmé's friend Emmanuel des Essarts wrote to Mallarmé of the literary world in 1868: "I see the younger poets at Lemerre's bookstore. They are charming and two-faced. . . . Verlaine looks sincere, but he has the endemic flaw of the lot of them: spiteful gossip. You can't imagine . . . how I suffer from all those stabs in the back and treacherous tongues."[7] The first, admiring letter Rimbaud wrote to Banville in 1870 and his departure, *en mauvaise odeur,* from Banville's residence in the fall of 1871 may be taken as the symbolic beginning and end of Rimbaud's navigation of the literary world. There remained, however, Verlaine: bored, bisexual, fearful of reprisals for continuing at his civil service post during the Commune, seemingly near the end of his literary gift—to judge from his none too recent latest work—basically directionless, and fundamentally *mal dans sa peau.* With him begins a new cycle in Rimbaud's life and art.

Chapter II

THE FALSE CONVERSION

I

The history of Rimbaud's poetry becomes especially problematic after his arrival in Paris in September 1871. By May 1872, the date of at least the copies of several poems, we not only know he was working in a new style, but we find a new thematic complex in his work which we shall eventually examine in detail. However, there is sound evidence that some poems were lost, and finally there is a striking poem, "Mémoire," written in a new style and perhaps the last piece in which Rimbaud used the alexandrine, but which remains curiously isolated in theme from the poems of May, June, and July 1872.

The very title "Mémoire" is significant of Rimbaud's new manner, for it contrasts with the nouns preceded by the definite article which he had so often used up to this point for titles and which suggest clearly conceived symbols or subjects of general reference. The poem has often been taken as autobiographical in import—referring to Rimbaud's parents—but the poem is not an enigma, as so specific an interpretation would make it: poems usually—and this is certainly true of Rimbaud's poetry—do not move in reference from general images to local, essentially uninteresting contingencies of the poet's past, but rather open onto larger perspectives. However, the larger perspective in this case does not concern time in the sense of general melancholy over its passage; it has reference to a historical framework.

The subject of "Mémoire" is actually one Rimbaud alludes to frequently in his work and which derives from Saint-Simonian or other Romantic social theories on woman's condition. There is, for example, a reference in *Une Saison en enfer* to the bourgeois materialism which makes modern marriage a union of partners in perpetual disagreement, a quite Balzacian topic. Elsewhere, in more discursive poems, "ces anciens ménages," that is, traditional marriages, are condemned, and the expression "l'amour est à réinventer" (*Une Saison en enfer*) does not refer to homosexuality, as some have pruriently supposed, but to the necessity for equality between the sexes. One poem of the Commune period, "Les Mains de Jeanne-Marie," is devoted to the new woman, in this case a revolutionary, a *pétroleuse*, whose dark hands are not the sign of some Spanish seductress, all Carmen and clichés, or those of the beaten-down factory worker or those of the housewife washing diapers. It is only with reference to the feminist theories which make up part of French Romantic social thought that one can understand the general tonality of disappointment and impatience associated with heterosexuality in poems like "Les Sœurs de charité," "Les Reparties de Nina," and "Mes Petites Amoureuses," all of which concern traditional conceptions of women.

The earliest references to women in Rimbaud's poetry, before his study of Romantic social theories, have agreeable connotations, as in "Sensation." The most significant of these early poems for Rimbaud's thought and for the thematic structure of "Mémoire" is "Soleil et chair," a piece of Parnassian imitation which one can too easily neglect because of its derivative style. Rimbaud, however, did not merely write on a borrowed theme which had no significance for him. "Soleil et chair" is his first cyclical poem; it deals with man and history and provided him with a basic scheme of ideas. In it we find a characteristic Romantic vision of paradise, fall, and redemption, but the cycle is anti-Christian, for paradise corresponds to sexuality in nature and ancient mythology, the fall to Christ's advent, and redemption will come about through a "renouveau d'amour," a return of erotic female deities. Meanwhile, man is shriveled and ugly. This way of accounting for the unsightliness of modern life even found its way into the poetry of the unpagan Baudelaire ("J'aime le souvenir") and shows the frequent parallelism of Romantic historical schemes to the Christian one, whether they are modified forms of it or completely opposed in spirit. We see a comparable tripartite scheme in the history of poetry included in the second *lettre du voyant*.

In "Mémoire" Rimbaud represents the original paradisiacal state of nature and man's fall into sexual disunion, but with such striking modernist poetic devices that one does not at first recognize that the underlying pattern is the Romantic one of "Soleil et chair," in its first and second stages. The first two parts of the poem represent, with extraordinary verbal virtuosity, a woman-river, against a vaguely medieval background, uniting with a male sun: this mythopoetic vision of sexuality in nature is technically unprecedented in French. Rimbaud then uses what is not so much a change of style as one of mode of representation: in Part III the female becomes an ironic modern "Madame" stepping on a flower, or despising nature, at which point the sun, still gloriously personified, vanishes over a mountain. Irony is followed by a brief elegiac note of lament for the sun's passing, as the imagery reverts in Part IV to the opening landscape. The disproportion between the haughty lady, with her parasol to ward off the male light, and the angel imagery used of the sun brilliantly renders what is almost the sexual irrelevance to each other of the male and female principles. Finally, another metamorphosis occurs: the profanation of natural sexuality takes the form of a gray, monotonous lake, with a disappointed old man sitting in a boat dredging for mud. The old man shows that the male principle, hitherto surrounded by imagery of glory, is also debased and impotent through the disunion of the sexes. The final word *boue* symbolizes the degradation of nature and human relations. The man's age and the progress in time from April to autumn suggest also the destructive natural cycle, the presence of time in a fallen or unilluminated world, which was ultimately to prove one of Rimbaud's most intimate preoccupations.

The interrelation of poems like "Soleil et chair," "Les Mains de Jeanne-Marie," and "Mémoire," of the observations on heterosexuality in *Une Saison en enfer* and in certain *Illuminations*, together with the remarks on breaking "l'infini servage de la femme" in the second *lettre du voyant*, are an excellent demonstration of the way images, myths, and ideology are elaborately connected in Rimbaud's thought. At the same time, he repeats himself very little; each stage in his poetic and intellectual development brings a different perspective to basic themes.

II

There is more than one phase of alienation in Rimbaud's thought and attitudes. The first is connected with or parallel to the political events of the spring of 1871: its most violent expression is found in "Paris se repeuple," dealing with the return to Paris of the bourgeoisie after the siege; in "Qu'est-ce pour nous, mon cœur"; in "Le Juste": and, of an erotic, nonpolitical nature, in "Mes Petites Amoureuses." These poems have always attracted less interest than the more soberly phrased ones of the same period, but they are particularly suggestive of the violent memories with which, in a stylized form, *Une Saison en enfer* opens.

A second phase of alienation set in after the break with the Paris literary men. Rimbaud's style was to reflect, even more than that of the poems just mentioned, the fact that he found "dérisoires les célébrités . . . de la poésie moderne" (*Une Saison en enfer*), for he turned away both from their modernism and from his own. He was now alienated not just from political adversaries, but virtually from the entire world. During this period Rimbaud confided in Verlaine alone, in Paris or by letter from Charleville, where he spent the early part of 1872. Solitude deeply affected his conception of the nature of poetry and of his destiny, and his old idea of the "long, immense et raisonné *dérèglement* de *tous les sens*" became more pertinent than it had been for poems like "Les Poètes de sept ans" or "Le Bateau ivre." Some careful analysis of this and related ideas is now relevant.

The derangement of the senses is ordinarily interpreted in an ahistorical, unphilosophical fashion counter to the facts of Rimbaud's poetry and of what we know of his life. In succinct form, this interpretation has it that Rimbaud, more or less constantly intoxicated with alcohol or drugs, produced great poetry which is essentially nonsense or, as it has been put in the finicky vocabulary of recent criticism, a "retrait du signifié."[1] One would think that enough students of Rimbaud's work had had the experience of being drunk to realize that it is a scarcely productive state, and as for drugs giving rise to poetry, that illusion is surely gone with the 1960s. Rimbaud drank a good deal, of course, in Verlaine's company especially, but so do countless people with no signs of poetry emanating from them, and the one time it is recorded that Rimbaud took hashish, he found the state it induced monotonous and annoying.[2] We are dealing here again with that often daft faith in experience that deranges the common sense of so many poetasters, critics, and philistines alike.

To analyze Rimbaud's famous phrase about the *dérèglement des sens*, we must recall what the 18th-century philosophers of the senses arrived at in their ponderings on such a puzzling phenomenon as perception, for, although Rimbaud's secular philosophical culture seems not to have been deep, he did know the outlines of Enlightenment philosophy. It was early recognized by those who theorized about the senses that it is a vulgar error to identify a sensation with some exterior thing which seems to cause it. As Jean-François de la Harpe put it:

If there is one irresistible demonstration, it is the one Locke worked out thoroughly, to the effect that there must be a faculty which perceives sensations and compares them. For it is physically proven that perception lies neither in objects nor in our senses. The odor is not in the flower, the coldness is not in the ice. . . . There is a faculty distinct from the senses which receives through them the impression of objects . . . and none of this, metaphysically speaking, has anything to do with matter.[3]

In other words, while the existence of the outer world is scarcely denied, our dependence on it for sensations is severely questioned. Our perceptions are not mechanical, any more than poetry is, and an earlier poet who was much concerned with 18th-century sensory philosophy, with the question of vision, and with the individual character of perception said:

"What," it will be Question'd, "When the Sun rises, do you not see a round disk of fire somewhat like a Guinea?" O no, no, I see an Innumerable company of the Heavenly host crying, "Holy, Holy, Holy . . . ."[4]

These delicate problems of poetic vision cannot be accounted for crudely by the gross explanation of drugs. When Rimbaud later turned against his visionary poetry of 1872, he spoke of it as coming about through the "hallucination of words," not by means of any intoxicant. Given that Rimbaud insists that the distortion of the senses is methodical and proceeds from theory ("raisonné") and observation ("JE est un autre"), and that the object is to arrive at some unknown area of the "plenitude of the great dream" or universal soul, we see that his conception is metaphysical, remote from any great faith in the material, and primarily spiritual in its intended results. It is the oversoul that supplies mental objects, according to the second *lettre du voyant*.

If we take the trouble to inquire, as far as it is possible, into how Rimbaud went about writing, we will find no intoxicated outpourings, but rather a highly intellectual insistence on work. "Work" is one of the key words running through Rimbaud's œuvre, and his letter to Delahaye from Paris in June 1872 provides an excellent suggestion of how it fitted into his life. He speaks of working all night in his room, meditating at dawn—his favorite hour—and then, as activity begins in the streets, going down to get drunk, have dinner, and return home to sleep. Except for the fact that he worked at night and had dinner in the morning, this working-day schedule is curiously like that of a great many people, although they may drink whiskey before dinner rather than absinth. As we look further into Rimbaud's writings, we find, besides the emphasis on hard work and the necessary "objectivity" of poetry in the *lettres du voyant*, that, in the midst of the disorderly life of the Foolish Virgin and her Infernal Spouse, they find time for "work." Rimbaud's poetry of 1872 is said, in *Une Saison*, to be the result of an *étude*, a *système*. The word "exercise" occurs in this connection in the drafts of *Une Saison*, and finally the word *science*, recurring through Rimbaud's writings, designates something that comes from meditation, study, and work. So we see that if we seriously examine Rimbaud in an intellectual, historical, and biographical context, we destroy the cherished image of the poet lying drunk in the gutter, improvising the *Illuminations*, an image attributable only to bad faith, fantasies of wish fulfillment, intellectual shallowness, pseudo-scholarship, or other vices on the part of Rimbaud's critics.

III

"La vieillerie poétique avait une bonne part dans mon alchimie du verbe." This remark, in *Une Saison en enfer*, refers to the poems of 1872 and is a particularly suggestive one, for, as I have noted, Rimbaud turned his back at once on the literary world, on its modernism, and on his own form of revolutionary modernism. "Opéras vieux, refrains niais, rythmes naïfs" are some of the terms Rimbaud uses to characterize the tones and forms he was working to adapt to his own poetry and which will constitute the basis of a new vision. From the scant Verlaine-Rimbaud correspondence of the spring of 1872, we know Rimbaud was led to a study of Favart's 18th-century opéra-comique librettos, which seemed to have influenced his prosody.[5] There is a further promising field of comparison as well in the opéra-ballet, the spectacular genre associated especially with Rameau and which Rimbaud may well have included in his designation "opéras vieux." Here we are dealing not with verbal echoes, but with the general tonality of poems. Rimbaud's "Bannières de mai" is a springtime plaint:

> Aux branches claires des tilleuls
> Meurt un maladif hallali.
> Mais des chansons spirituelles
> Voltigent parmi les groseilles.
>
> .   .   .   .
> Le ciel est joli comme un ange.
> L'azur et l'onde communient.
> Je sors. Si un rayon me blesse
> Je succomberai sur la mousse.
>
> Qu'on patiente et qu'on s'ennuie
> C'est trop simple. Fi de mes peines.
> Je veux que l'été dramatique
> Me lie à son char de fortune.
> Que par toi beaucoup, ô Nature,
> —Ah! moins seul et moins nul!—je meurs.
> Au lieu que les Bergers, c'est drôle,
> Meurent à peu près par le monde.

(In the bright branches of the linden trees, a sickly death cry grows faint. But spiritual canticles bound through the gooseberries. . . . The sky is pretty as an angel. The blue sky and blue sea commune. I go out. If a sunbeam wounds me, I shall succumb on the moss. It is too simple for me merely to suffer and be wretched. Enough of my troubles! I want dramatic summer to bind me to her chariot of fortune. O Nature, let me die immensely through you—less alone and null! Whereas shepherds, it's funny, die more or less throughout the world.)

This is a spiritual version of the springtime plaint, in which Rimbaud deliberately suggests the conventionalized, attenuated language of old-fashioned operatic poetry by the clichés "joli comme un ange," "fi de mes peines," and "char de fortune," and by the lover's aspiration towards death. As a Neoclassical analogue, we can take these lines from Rameau's *Les Amours champêtres*:

> Ces tendres fleurs qui parent la verdure,
> Ont parfumé l'haleine des Zéphyrs,

De ce beau jour la lumière est plus pure.

.   .   .   .

Quand le Printemps ranime la Nature,
Moi seul, hélas, j'expire de langueur;
Mais prends pitié des peines que j'endure,
Et le Printemps va naître dans mon cœur.

(These tender flowers bedecking the green have scented the zephyrs' breath; the light of this beautiful day is purer. When Spring brings Nature back to life, I alone, alas, am dying of languor. But take pity on the suffering I endure, and Spring will be born in my heart.)

All is, of course, cliché in Rameau's libretto, but it is not enough simply to dismiss such verse as hackneyed. Rimbaud particularized his imagery more than Neoclassical poets did, but he recuperated an effect he found in this kind of diction: the unemphaticness of the language and the preference for images of the light and radiant have a spiritualizing quality, as if the lover were not really flesh and blood. Rimbaud is trying to render the experience of a soul sloughing off matter: all is sun, breeze, and canticles addressed to the soul, which will ascend beyond its mortal prison. Looking at Neoclassical verse from the vantage point of Rimbaud's own earlier poems, with their violent color and intense imagery of the material, we see how such soft language, naïve and faded in comparison with 19th-century poetry, has the charm of a pastoral world where suffering is attenuated and exquisite.

One of the poems of 1872 whose imagery most suggests some filiation from the opéra-ballet is "Bonne Pensée du matin." The poem opens with a pastoral movement evoked in Rameau's *Tircis et Doristée*:

Paresseuse Aurore,
Tu ne parois point encore!
Plein d'un feu qui me dévore
Je devance ton réveil.
Tout dans cet asyle
Est encore tranquille,
Et mes yeux seuls
Sont privés de sommeil.

A quatre heures du matin, l'été,
Le sommeil d'amour dure encore.
Sous les bosquets l'aube évapore
L'odeur du soir fêté.

(Indolent Dawn, you have not appeared yet! Full of a devouring fire, I am up before you. Everything in this idyllic spot is still quiet, and my eyes alone are sleepless.)

(At four in the morning in summer, love's sleep still lasts. In the groves, dawn evaporates the scent of the evening's festivities.)

Next Rimbaud refers to the busy workers:

> Mais là-bas dans l'immense chantier
> Vers le soleil des Hespérides,
> En bras de chemise, les charpentiers
> Déjà s'agitent.

(But in the distance, in the immense shipyard, in the direction of the Hesperides' sun, the carpenters in shirtsleeves are already busy.)

The Hesperides are, of course, associated with the west, not the east: Rimbaud is merely making jargon in imitation of Neoclassical poetry. As for the shipyard workers, they are not common Europeans, but exotic inhabitants of Babylon, as it soon becomes clear. The more spectacular opéras-ballets had choruses of all kinds of picturesque people: fisherfolk, pirates, sailors, Turks, shepherds, Persians, American Indians, and so forth. In *Les Indes galantes*, Rameau's most famous work, there is an especially great variety of such figures.

Venus is invoked in regard to the workers:

> Ah! pour ces Ouvriers charmants
> Sujets d'un roi de Babylone,
> Vénus! laisse un peu les Amants,
> Dont l'âme est en couronne.

(Ah, for these charming workmen, subjects of a king of Babylon, Venus! leave for a moment the lovers whose souls' desires are crowned.)

Babylonian workmen are obviously more colorful figures than ordinary shipbuilders, but there is more coherence here than may at first appear. Babylon was indeed a sea power, and its most prominent and enduring deity was Astarte, identified with Venus, who, furthermore, as Aphrodite Pelagia, was associated with the sea. The invocation to Venus or similar figures is a common genre in the opéra-ballet, like this one:

> Grâces, quittez Cythère,
> Venez sur ce gazon
> Pour danser et pour plaire.
> Venez de la Bergère
> Prendre leçon.
>   (*Les Festes d'Hébé*)

(Graces, leave Venus' isle, come to this lawn to dance and please men. Come learn from the Shepherdess.)

"Bonne Pensée du matin" can be seen as an attempt to transmute conventionalized material from 18th-century opera into a delicately fantastic version of pastoral that retains a suggestion of the old-fashioned while avoiding the actual clichés of earlier poetic language. This land of *fêtes d'amour* and workers as mythological as gnomes is a fine example of the deranged and visionary senses creating a vivid supernatural impression on the basis of texts and conventions which are part of the byways of literature and play no role in the history of high art.

In "Est-elle almée" the references to the Fisherwoman and the Pirate suggest the characters of the interludes of the opéra-ballet; the word *fête* in the poem, often used in the titles of Rameau's works, as well as in the poems of 1872, further suggests the stage, as does the illusory spectacle of the oriental dancer, the *almée*, in the night, before dawn and humble folk close the scene.

IV

Rimbaud does not imitate older poems in the ordinary sense of pastiche, but rather alludes to the existence of such genres. With the fairy tale, however, there is no question of even approximate verbal echoes such as the mythological invocation. Furthermore, the source of fairy-tale material is double: the often ironic literary fairy tale of the 18th century and the vastly popular theatrical genre known as the *féerie*. In respect to the latter, we have Delahaye's word that Rimbaud was attracted to it;[6] it seems difficult to imagine, however, that Rimbaud was not also well acquainted with the literary fairy tale. In any case, both genres invited a certain ironic enjoyment. But since the theatrical *féerie* has such a peculiar place in the history of stage entertainment, a few words about it are appropriate.

We can scarcely imagine today the enormous popularity in the 19th century of *féeries*. These adult magical spectacles included both stories drawn from Perrault's fairy tales and made-up ones. What distinguished this *théâtre du silence*, as it has been called, was its handling of causality: in this utterly non-Aristotelian genre, seemingly incoherent series of tableaux were common; a flouting of rational causality was taken as a matter of course. The sense of the unreal was assumed to be as important as the sense of the real in high art, and the *merveilleux* was its dynamic. In this unphilosophical representation of the supernatural, serious themes like fate, the struggle of good and evil, guilt, failure, and the presence of ominous forces were given a light or naïve character, masking somewhat their sinister character. The naïveté was, of course, thoroughly self-conscious, like that of the literary fairy tale. Often self-consciousness became so overt that the result was the frankly burlesque *féerie*. The major literary work that the French assimilated to the *féerie* was *A Midsummer Night's Dream*, which Rimbaud later drew upon for "Bottom" in the *Illuminations*.[7]

Rimbaud's adaptation of the conventions of the *féerie* is nicely illustrated by "Jeune Ménage":

La chambre est ouverte au ciel bleu-turquin;
Pas de place: des coffrets et des huches!
Dehors le mur est plein d'aristoloches
Où vibrent les gencives des lutins.

Que ce sont bien intrigues de génies
Cette dépense et ces désordres vains!
C'est la fée africaine qui fournit
La mûre, et les résilles dans les coins.

Plusieurs entrent, marraines mécontentes,
En pans de lumière dans les buffets,
Puis y restent! le ménage s'absente
Peu sérieusement, et rien ne se fait.

(The chamber is open to the turquoise sky. There is no room: trunks and chests! Outside, the wall is covered with birthwort vibrating with sprites' gums. It certainly looks like jinns have been at work: so much money spent and such pointless disorder! The African fairy provides the mulberries and spiderwebs in corners. Several none-too-pleased godmothers enter the sideboards on beams of light, then stay. The couple has gone out rather frivolously, and nothing gets done.)

In and around this half medieval, half fantastic cottage there is a whole array of supernatural creatures. We gather that the wayward young couple has been led astray by jinns and an African fairy, of whose activities the fairy godmothers disapprove. At first the quarrel seems merely a matter of domestic economy and poor housekeeping (the *résilles* or "nets" in the corners must be spiderwebs), but the word "intrigue" hints at some greater struggle for power. The spectacular surface of the action somewhat conceals the real question of plot: such is the nature of the *féerie.* In any case, things grow clearly worse:

Le marié a le vent qui le floue
Pendant son absence, ici, tout le temps.
Même des esprits des eaux, malfaisants
Entrent vaguer aux sphères de l'alcôve.

La nuit, l'amie oh! la lune de miel
Cueillera leur sourire et remplira
De mille bandeaux de cuivre le ciel.
Puis ils auront affaire au malin rat.

(The husband is being cheated here by the wind, all the time during his absence. Even evil water sprites come in and wander in the circles of the bed nook. At night, their friend, oh, the honeymoon, will pluck their smile and fill the sky with a thousand copper bands. Then they will have to deal with the sly rat.)

Not only is the couple wasteful, but they are being deceived, and their cottage taken over. Their friend the moon will provide an extraordinary display in the evening, but that will not prevent the inevitable confrontation with evil forces. Some higher saving power, however, may appear:

> —S'il n'arrive pas un feu follet blême,
> Comme un coup de fusil, après des vêpres.
> —O spectres saints et blancs de Bethléem,
> Charmez plutôt le bleu de leur fenêtre!

(Unless a pale ignis fatuus appears, like a gunshot, after vespers. O holy white ghosts of Bethlehem, enchant, rather, their blue window!)

Christian material appears in an attenuated, folkloric form, and the Holy Family is asked to cast a spell. We sense the drama of all this, but we cannot define the situation fully. There is a kind of brilliant economy in the poem by which we enjoy the general effect of the *féerie* and its plot tensions without being burdened with tedious detail: this is a quintessential version of the *féerie*.

The tendency the *féerie* had to become a chaotic spectacle is Rimbaud's justification for cutting out exact causal links and offering us more the hint of a plot than a realized one. Juxtaposition without explicit causality is the method of "Bruxelles":

> Plate-bandes d'amarantes jusqu'à
> L'agréable palais de Jupiter.
> —Je sais que c'est *Toi*, qui, dans ces lieux,
> Mêles ton Bleu presque de Sahara!

(Beds of amaranthus as far as Jupiter's pleasant palace. You are the one, I know, who mingle your almost Saharan blue in these skies!)

Here we have a mysterious power (is *Toi* the same as Jupiter?), and the city is metamorphosed into a magic garden. In it the past comes to life, a fairy-tale motif:

> —Calmes maisons, anciennes passions!
> Kiosques de la Folle par affection.
> Après les fesses des rosiers, balcon
> Ombreux et très-bas de la Juliette.
>
> .   .   .   .
>
> Banc vert où chante au paradis d'orage
> Sur la guitare, la blanche Irlandaise.

(Calm houses, old passions! Summerhouse of the woman mad from love. After the rose branches, Juliet's very low shadowy balcony.... A green bench where in the storm paradise the white Irish lady sings with her guitar.)

The *folle* here seems to be Juana la Loca, the 15th-century queen of Spain and Flanders, who spent part of her life in what is now Belgium; Shakespeare's Juliet and Yseut as well make their appearances. The last stanza stresses that this is the *féerie*, the *théâtre du silence*:

> —Boulevard sans mouvement ni commerce,
> Muet, tout drame et toute comédie,

Réunion des scènes infinies,
Je te connais et t'admire en silence.

(Boulevard void of business and movement, silent, nothing but melodrama and theater, the meeting place of a thousand scenes, I know you and admire you without
speaking.)

The mingling of the spiritual world of the past with the natural world is
part of the effect which partakes at once of the theatrical illusion, of the
spell (note the word *charmez* in "Jeune Ménage") or *sophisme magique*
(the term is from *Une Saison*), and of a vision of metaphysical forces, like
the rat opposed to the ghosts of Bethlehem dressed in Mary's blue and
white. In "Michel et Christine" apocalyptic images of a "religious" storm
and of red, white, and black warriors end in a burlesque idyll. The title
and some slight reference come from a *mélodrame* by Scribe about a soldier returning from the wars. Rimbaud borrows from and emphasizes the
frankly artificial character of 19th-century popular theater.

Stylization is a form of spiritualization in these poems. Matter becomes
tenuous, fanciful, and images of light dominate, as causality vanishes: all
the scientific, materialistic bonds of the real world disappear in a vision of
metaphysical reality. The naïve represents a refusal of the contingent bur-
dens of modern life and the revolutionary struggle. Evil is not a terrible
darkness, but is represented by strange, *fantasque* figures like the rat in
"Jeune Ménage" or the crippled peasant of "La Rivière de Cassis." As we
explore the metaphysics of Rimbaud's visionary poetry, the peculiarly
accessory, subordinate character of evil points towards some important
aspects of this verse, as well as does the curious blending of pathos and
irony, strongest perhaps in "Honte."

In theological terms, what is called the order of nature has been transformed. The natural world, which in Rimbaud's earliest poetry serves the
ideological role of a foil to bourgeois society and war ("Le Dormeur du
val"), a symbol of freedom in the revolutionary effort, is not very clearly
accounted for in the *lettres du voyant*, for Rimbaud had not yet cast off his
imagery of a firm, brilliantly colored, and highly material universe. Now,
with the deepening of his perceptual *dérèglement*, the order of nature will
join the order of grace, in contradiction to the theological tradition. Saints
appear in the moonlit pea vines of "Entends comme brame," Christ as
Pascal Lamb among the flocks of "Michel et Christine," and Saint Anne
is invoked as part of the "Fêtes de la faim." Plaintiveness and buffoonery
join.

The significant word *philtre* occurs in "Entends comme brame," intro-
ducing the theme of drinking and eating, which (as in Holy Communion)
will most strongly link nature and grace. "La Rivière de Cassis," for example, describes a cleftlike valley, a sacred spot with restoring waters for the

passing pilgrim. In it the wind (the spiritus or breath of God as over the waters in Genesis), which is virtually a new image in Rimbaud's vocabulary in 1872, will cover the murmur of the battles of good and evil fought by the knights errant.[8] Medieval references (the knights were probably suggested by those apocalyptic figures in Hugo's *La Légende des siècles*) bear religious overtones, as in the "Sicile, Allemagne" of "Entends comme brame," which designates the *Holy* Roman Empire of the early 13th century.

Ghosts and specters, so numerous in these pieces of 1872, are, however, absent from two important poems on spiritual thirst, a Biblical metaphor (e.g., Matthew 5:6 or I Corinthians 10:4) with a long literary history. The first, "Comédie de la soif," continuing the effect of theater with its dialogue and choruses, deals with the pilgrim unsatisfied with earthly drink. The "Green Inn" of nature is his goal, but instead of actually drinking, he longs to dissolve amid damp, dawnlit flowers. Likewise, in the prayer "Le loup criait," the theme is asceticism, the refusal of physical nourishment and the desire to become a broth on Solomon's altar. One naïve song, "Fêtes de la faim," is about eating stones, that is, doing away with obstacles to spiritual progress by ignoring the body's needs.

The *fête*, comedy, and prayer are all ceremonious, and in the fourth of Rimbaud's drinking poems, "Larme," a ritual is evoked. Rituals commemorate or induce metaphysical events, and here there is an attempt to achieve communion with the divine through drinking gold (besides the usual symbolism of gold in Rimbaud—sun, golden age—there is an ancient cordial, *aurum potabile*, which regenerates its drinker). The version of the poem given in *Une Saison en enfer* is tighter than the first one; isolated from the idyll of flocks, village girls, and birds, the poet seeks the true drink:

> Que pouvais-je boire dans cette jeune Oise,
> —Ormeaux sans voix, gazon sans fleurs, ciel couvert!—
> Boire à ces gourdes jaunes, loin de ma case
> Chérie? Quelque liqueur d'or qui fait suer.

(What could I drink in this young river—birdless elms, flowerless turf, sultry sky—drink in these yellow gourds, far from my dear hut? Some golden liquid that makes you sweat.)

Neither the spring (the headwaters of the Oise) nor the exotic fruit (the word *case* also suggests something of the exotic opera interlude) provides true gold, but only what appears to be beer. The *spiritus Dei* and apocalyptic storm (another new symbol in these 1872 poems, used also in "Michel et Christine") rise, as the speaker is bent over, perhaps like some awkward picture of the drinker on an inn sign:

> Je faisais une louche enseigne d'auberge.
> —Un orage vint chasser le ciel. Au soir

L'eau des bois se perdait sur les sables vierges,
Le vent de Dieu jetait des glaçons aux mares;

Pleurant, je voyais de l'or—et ne pus boire.—

(I looked like a peculiar inn sign. A storm drove away the clouds. In the evening, the water from the woods trickled away on the virgin sand; God's wind threw icicles into the ponds; weeping I saw gold—and could not drink.)

The ritual ends in failure, in some check which prevents the attainment of the divine. The sense of failure is not unrelated to the irony about the vision of saints in "Entends comme brame," the burlesque character of Christ's appearance in "Michel et Christine," the plaintiveness of the end of "Comédie de la soif," or the resignation of "Bannières de mai." Everywhere we feel that the poet's attempt to absorb himself totally in this visionary world is countered by the irony or melancholy of not being able to make of it his true life. It is in this failure that we see the dualism implicit in the poems of 1872: there is an unhappy lower level of life from which the poet is not able completely to escape. However, there is an even greater effort made to achieve a visionary life than the ones commemorated by the poems we have seen. Rimbaud's verse of 1872 culminates in a series of lyrics using the mystics' images of the tower, the castle, and the vision of eternity.

V

The word *patience*, new in Rimbaud's vocabulary in 1872, occurs in "Comédie de la soif" and indicates the waiting and suffering (*patior*) which attend experiences like that described in "Larme." With "Fêtes de la patience," we reach the high point of Rimbaud's cycle of poems of spiritual aspiration—since he himself arranged them as a cycle in *Une Saison en enfer*, we are justified in seeing such a shape in them. The first of these poems, "Bannières de mai," we have already looked at. The others have more marked analogies with verse in the mystic tradition. The subject of the "Chanson de la plus haute tour" is the poet's having wasted his youth by his excessive concern for idle matters and other people ("Oisive jeunesse, / A tout asservie, / Par délicatesse / J'ai perdu ma vie"); the only possible spiritual salvation lies in retreat, in turning one's back on the world:

Je me suis dit: laisse,
Et qu'on ne te voie:
Et sans la promesse
De plus hautes joies.
Que rien ne t'arrête,
Auguste retraite.

(I told myself stop! have nothing to do with others, and until you are certain of the highest joys, let nothing put an end to your august retreat.)

The general aspiration and a key term of the "Chanson" are to be found in the poetry of a 17th-century French mystic:

> Tout pour Dieu, rien pour soi; car le moi n'étant plus,
> Rien ne trouble et rien n'inquiète,
> Quitte des pensers superflus,
> En Dieu l'âme fait sa retraite.

(All for God, nothing for the self, for when the *I* is no more, nothing disturbs or disquiets us; free of superfluous thoughts, the soul makes its retreat in God.)

This is from the *Poésies et cantiques spirituels* of Jeanne Guyon, the notorious exponent of Quietism, whose verse was at one time quite famous.[9] Obviously Madame Guyon felt herself to be an orthodox Christian and consequently talks very specifically about God, whereas Rimbaud's thought had detached itself from orthodoxy to the point that he avoided the word "God," although references to the Virgin Mary, Christ, and Saint Anne occur in passing in the poems of 1872. We can also compare a passage in Madame Guyon's work with Rimbaud's "L'Eternité," the cosmological vision, which is far more light and airy than in "Le Bateau ivre":

> Elle est retrouvée.
> Quoi? —L'Eternité.
> C'est la mer allée
> Avec le soleil.

(It has been found. What? Eternity. It is the sea stretching out under the sun.)

Madame Guyon speaks more discursively of the infinite ocean and eternity; she does not conflate time and space:

> Dans cet espace immense
> De l'Océan divin
> Je fais ma résidence
> Dans l'amour souverain:
> Là rien ne me surcharge.
> Tout est mon lieu
> Aiant trouvé le large
> Dedans mon Dieu.
>   (I, 145)

> Lors son lieu c'est Dieu même,
> Son tems l'éternité;
> Son bien est sa misère extrême;
> Sa foiblesse est sa fermeté.
>   (II, 132)

(In the immense space of the divine ocean I take up my abode, in sovereign love: there nothing weighs on me. Every place is mine, since I have found the open sea within God. Then the soul's place is God himself, his time eternity; his wealth is his great wretchedness; his weakness is his strength.)

A part of the mystic quest made famous by the works of Saint John of the Cross is the Dark Night, which, once passed through, vanishes into insignificance:

> Ame sentinelle
> Murmurons l'aveu
> De la nuit si nulle
> Et du jour en feu.

(My soul on watch, let us murmur our recognition of night's nullity and the fiery day.)

The ambiguity of the fire of love, searing yet ecstatic, is alluded to by Madame Guyon as she also speaks of the Dark Night:

> Le feu, tous ses tourments, ordonnés par l'Amour
> Sont des lieux remplis de délices;
> Il faut changer la nuit en jour,
> Tournant en plaisirs les supplices.
>
> (I, 14)

(The fire and all its torments ordained by love are places filled with delight. You must change the night into day, turning torture into pleasure.)

Generally Madame Guyon, in keeping with Quietist theory, emphasizes passivity and the idea of pleasure. The notion of compulsion and rigor in the mystic experience is stronger in Rimbaud:

> Puisque de vous seules,
> Braises de satin,
> Le Devoir s'exhale
> Sans qu'on dise: enfin.

(Since from you alone, satin embers, breathes spiritual duty, to which one never says: enough.)

One sees the connection with the whole complex of ideas of work, *dérègle-ment raisonné,* and the duty of cultivating one's soul, which we find in the second *lettre du voyant.* Rimbaud's fire is harsher, and Madame Guyon's use of the notion of duty is characteristically a passive one:

> Que chacun apprenne
> A ne rien vouloir,
> Afin qu'il comprenne
> La loi du devoir;

> Et que son cœur
> Soit souple à son Moteur.
> (I, 100)

(Let each learn to want nothing, in order that he learn the law of duty, and let his heart respond to its Mover.)

(The *sixain* of this last poem is especially reminiscent of the verse form of the "Chanson de la plus haute tour.")

Patience and suffering, even though their connotations may be somewhat different, are linked in both poets:

> Là pas d'espérance,
> Nul orietur.
> Science avec patience,
> Le supplice est sûr.

(There is no hope there, no new sunrise; knowledge with suffering, the torment is certain.)

The key term *science*, the possession of the supreme Savant of the second *lettre du voyant*, designates something arrived at by "torture," "toute la foi, toute la force surhumaine." Again we see greater passivity in Madame Guyon:

> Je veux que la souffrance
> Ne le rebute pas,
> Qu'en la plus longue patience,
> Il ne se sente jamais las.
> (I, 71)

(I want him not to be repelled by suffering; I want him never to feel weary even in the longest endurance.)

Finally, we encounter the notions of the "august" retreat, the dark night, knowledge, and vast space—themes Rimbaud divides up—coming together in Madame Guyon's verse:

> Plus vaste que les cieux est cette sombre nuit,
> Toujours consacrée au silence;
> Eloigné du monde et du bruit,
> On apprend l'auguste science.
> (I, 174)

(Vaster than the skies is this dark night, forever given over to silence. For far from the world and its noise, we learn august knowledge.)

In "Age d'or," the last of the "Fêtes de la patience," the poet sees a castle, the symbol of spiritual attainment, and an angel explains that nature is the poet's family, just as the sun had been a parent in "Bannières de mai."

The "vicious world" must be forgotten, and all misfortune consumed in fire. This is the end of the quest, the "chemin de croix" Rimbaud told Verlaine they were to lead, in a letter of the spring of 1872.

It is worth exploring the theological background of these poems, for, although Rimbaud's knowledge of the history of dogma was surely limited, he had been a first-rate student in religious studies at the Collège de Charleville and was thoroughly acquainted with basic concepts of theology. He was probably aware, from his Biblical readings, and especially from Saint John, the most theological and exciting of the evangelists, that the doctrine of original sin has no basis in the gospels: "Behold what manner of love the Father hath bestowed upon us that we should be called the sons of God"; "Whosoever is born of God does not commit sin, for his seed remaineth in him: and he cannot sin, because he is born of God" (I John 3:1, 9).[10] This doctrine, radical-seeming in the context of 19th-century dogmatic Catholicism, was specifically developed by the heresiarch Pelagius, whom Augustine combatted in one of the most famous episodes in theological history. Pelagius believed that perfect grace was obtainable in life, that the order of grace can be identified with the order of nature. The Eastern Church, for its part, maintained that mysticism ends in deification.[11] Closer to Rimbaud's own time, the Quietist heresy, of Spanish baroque origin, held that favored souls had a passive receptiveness to the Word of God and bypassed confession, Church, and Christ in their attainment of perfection through elimination of selfhood. It is hard to estimate what Rimbaud might have taken from the history of theology as opposed to his own original recreations of theological problems. We must understand, nonetheless, that his themes fit very much into the traditional framework of theological concerns.

Rimbaud's theology, however, is less a series of abstract propositions than a living, dramatic sequence of thoughts arranged in the pattern of a quest. The dominant means of the quest is the Word or revelation. All words can become the Word in Rimbaud's view of creative language, similar to Hugo's, and the poem becomes a ritual—indeed, Madame Guyon's songs also seem intended to induce Quietist feelings of selflessness and perfection. To point out again that the power of the Word is not a vain imagining, Rimbaud's Word lay at the origins of Verlaine's orthodox conversion, for until his association with Rimbaud, Verlaine had been a free-thinker and skeptic. Again we must emphasize that words are experience and knowledge. The Word produces metaphysical events, and so, looking back on this period in his life, Rimbaud considered it an attempt at salvation through language. The Word transformed nature into radiance ("God is light," says Saint John), and much of the imagery of nature in the 1872 poems tends towards an airy sort of dematerialization of brightness.

With "Age d'or," we reach the climax of "Fêtes de la patience," a sequence which appears complete in itself and wonderfully rich in themes and images. However, the comedy of "Age d'or," with its poet, angel and chorus, does not constitute a true conclusion, for the cyclic turning movement so characteristic of Rimbaud's imagination is embodied in what is thematically the final piece of the poems of 1872, the great "O saisons, ô châteaux." This elliptical, irregularly versified poem suggests in its refrain words, "castles" and "seasons," the peculiar theological cast of mind of the poems of 1872: castles are a traditional symbol of spiritual elevation, while the word "seasons" evokes the way nature participates in the order of grace.

The vocabulary of "O saisons, ô châteaux" is not solely important, however, in the refrain words. We find here the complement to the Word or ritual poetry, which is physical ascesis, with its peculiar features that run through the poems of 1872, suggesting a rigorous trial in which body is the object of contempt. The *patience* or suffering, "toutes les formes de la souffrance," mentioned in the second *lettre du voyant*, will now balance the ascensional movement of the spirit. "O saisons, ô châteaux" describes aspiration, an obscure, menacing turning point, and finally the failure of the quest; the poem introduces the notion of *bonheur*, meaning at once "happiness" in the profane sense of satisfaction and "beatitude" in keeping with the theological use of *bonheur*. We are here in the presence of a truly rich ambiguity. Equally evocative in this poem are the allusions to sodomy and magic, which qualify the notion of *bonheur* and give it so strange and pathetic a resonance. So far Rimbaud has remained in the mainstream of ascetic thought, but now he goes beyond it, as he introduces magic and sodomy as part of the complex of salvation, *bonheur*, and absorption of the body into a higher state:

> O saisons, ô châteaux
> Quelle âme est sans défauts?
>
> O saisons, ô châteaux
>
> J'ai fait la magique étude
> Du Bonheur, que nul n'élude.
>
> O vive lui, chaque fois
> Que chante son coq gaulois.
>
> Mais! je n'aurai plus d'envie,
> Il s'est chargé de ma vie.
>
> Ce Charme! il prit âme et corps,
> Et dispersa tous efforts.

(O seasons, O castles! What soul is without flaw? I have made the magic study of blessedness, which no one can avoid. A salute to him every time his Gallic cock sings. But

I will have no more desires; he has taken charge of my life. This spell! —it has taken body and soul and dispelled all effort.)

It would be out of keeping with Rimbaud's inspiration at this time to take the reference to sodomy merely as a kind of dirty joke—which is what at least one editor does—for sodomy has a long association with magic, going back to medieval views of sorcery. Verlaine called it "l'affranchissement de la lourde nature"—an escape from lower nature—and stressed the metaphysical dimensions of sodomy ("Un grand inconnu m'entoure") in a sexually explicit sonnet contemporary with Rimbaud's last verse poems; this is "Le Bon Disciple" (May 1872), in which intimations of beatitude join with bestial postures. Furthermore, there is an old heretical tradition of orgies as rites of purification which it was scarcely above Rimbaud's capacties to recreate. The peculiarity in all this is that sodomy appears not as a particular subservience to the physical, but as a means of ascension, a kind of spiritual exercise. Its connotations are ascetic; it has a negative relation to the body, and this is in keeping with the whole denial of material limitations in the *dérèglement de tous les sens*.

When one tries to penetrate the significance of sodomy for Rimbaud, the notion turns out to be ambiguous, since, as we follow "O saisons, ô châteaux," we discover that magic, beatitude, and homosexuality fail; their fragile synthesis in a pseudo-mystic theology reveals its weakness as soon as it is affirmed, and we encounter the turning point of the cycle, so typical of Rimbaud's imagination. First of all, words suddenly lose their meaning:

> Que comprendre à ma parole?
> Il fait qu'elle fuie et vole.
>
> O saisons, ô châteaux!

(What can I make of my words? He makes them rise and fly. O seasons, O castles!)

A greater obscurity of reference in the pronouns and possessive adjectives in this poem implies a certain dissolution of the vision, an inability to grasp it completely. The logos or spell is vanishing into what Rimbaud calls disparagingly a "hallucination of words" (*Une Saison*). The supernatural dimensions of the reasoned-out *dérèglement des sens* now appear as sheer uncontrolled verbalism. And as the logos was the instrument of salvation, its disappearance casts the poet back into the profane word.

The expression "Quelle âme est sans défauts?" at the beginning of "O saisons, ô châteaux" suggests a further curious side to the poems of 1872: in the absence of any concept of original sin, we nevertheless find words like *infortune, malheur*, and abundant suggestions of unhappiness. This peculiar version of the mystical quest, which would end in the universal soul, did not succeed:

Et, si le malheur m'entraîne,
Sa disgrâce m'est certaine.

Il faut que son dédain, las!
Me livre au plus prompt trépas!

—O Saisons, ô Châteaux!

(And if misfortune tears me away, my disgrace in his eyes is certain. His disdain, alas, must give me over to immediate death. O seasons, O castles!)

Death lay at the end of the ascetic absorption into pure light, and when Rimbaud recognized this, he wrote *Une Saison en enfer*, as, in part, the record of what he calls in the drafts his "false conversion." What had appeared as the promise of a total immersion in an otherworldly spiritual life involved the extinction of both body and spirit in death, for instead of unity the poet finds dualism, a dualism which is covertly suggested by the chain of references to this-worldly wretchedness. A hallucination of words and bodily deterioration was all that Rimbaud's "eternal life" consisted of. "Escaping from reality" (the latter a rare word in Rimbaud) seems also to have led to great tension and outbursts of physical violence, if we can take the "Délires" I section of *Une Saison* as having any literal autobiographical value. In other words, Rimbaud was living on two planes. To begin with, the poems of distorted perception, of seeing into the universal soul, were complemented by those which could be best described as spiritual exercises. This kind of angelism or aspiration to unity and identity with the universal soul imposed a strenuous mental effort, suggested by the title of the lost "La Chasse spirituelle," with its implications of pursuit and perhaps perpetual longing and unsatisfaction. On the plane of everyday life, however, Rimbaud apparently lacked the calm and cheerfulness often remarked on in the famous mystics. "Un paradis de tristesse," says the Foolish Virgin of her life with the Infernal Spouse, and the description of the latter, a brilliant retrospective self-portrait, which Rimbaud then filtered through the consciousness and character of the Foolish Virgin, suggests a sometimes frantic desire to transcend the conditions of life, which results in hostility and quarrelsomeness.

Before examining Rimbaud's own theological criticism of his poems of 1872 and of his life around that year, we should try to assess his thought without the prejudices of *Une Saison en enfer* coloring our attempt. The question of Rimbaud's "mysticism" is most easily disposed of: he seems to have assimilated some of the language of mysticism and the notion of mysticism as a discipline to his idea of perceptual disordering; the result might best be called visionary, since words pertaining to sight dominate the *lettres du voyant*. Nothing about the unfolding of Rimbaud's life in 1872 or after suggests any serious analogy with the career of the great mystics. Mystical poetry, which he encountered perhaps in Madame Guyon's work—the most likely hypothesis, to my mind—lent a distinctive coloring to his work, like the other *vieilleries poétiques* he studied, but one which is distorted by his own theological bias. Most notably, the idea of union with the One, so characteristic of mysticism, is lacking in his thought: mystical thinking, as in its Neoplatonic form, tends to conceive of a point of irradiation of the universe, of a focus which could be called God, which invites contemplation, and with which the mystic ultimately merges.

There is, however, a certain resemblance between Rimbaud's thought and Neoplatonism, whether in its pagan, occultist, or semi-Christian forms: the insistence on light, on the casting off of the body and matter, on the relegation of evil to a subsidiary, contingent place, and on immersion in the world soul are present, although we do not see a chain of being or hierarchy running from matter to God, as in Victor Hugo's rather Neoplatonic occultism. (A good deal of Rimbaud's thought, of course, could be derived from Saint John's Gospel and Epistles.) At the same time, the notion of deification seems especially strong: the poet—"moi qui me suis dit mage ou ange"—has a vision of becoming one among a throng of Godless angels in "Age d'or." These angels, the Christian holy figures, the exotic apparitions, the saints, and the specters form an imagery expressive of the otherworldly oversoul and constitute the element of creative theology in Rimbaud's vision. Such imagery is a remarkable achievement in syncretism and synthesis, like the mythologies of Gérard de Nerval and Blake: the more one studies these curious poems of 1872, the more impressive this phase of Rimbaud's poetic and theological evolution begins to seem. Notions of the world soul can be abstract and devoid of emotive coloring, or the world soul can be conceived of as immanent and free of any connotations of supernaturalism, as in certain Romantics. However, Rimbaud's otherworld soul gives rise to superreal images of a particular brightness and detail, the content of the *dérèglement des sens*, which conveys a strange vision appearing through natural phenomena, as it were. There is a superimposition of the spiritual upon the ordinary. This vision is all the more fascinating for the poet's frequent sense of check, irony, inability to fix it, and the reminder that

> L'heure de sa fuite, hélas!
> Sera l'heure du trépas.
>
> O saisons, ô châteaux!

(The hour of his flight, alas, will be the hour of death. O seasons, O castles!)

VI

Verlaine was, of course, the only witness to Rimbaud's changing conceptions, and one of his more remarkable poems, "Crimen Amoris," is devoted to portraying, in symbolic form, Rimbaud's theology, as it appeared to one headed towards orthodoxy. (Verlaine's poem was completed in July or August 1873, just after his incarceration, and he therefore did not yet know the final form of *Une Saison en enfer*, which was finished in August.) The religious theme first appears in Verlaine's work in one poem of *Romances sans paroles*, where the poet compares himself to a Christian martyr; then such themes grow stronger in "Luxures," a poem about homosexuality and the theological enigma of the flesh (*luxure* and *chair* have strong liturgical associations),[12] and two or three other sonnets apparently dating from the spring of 1873. Wé see in "Luxures," by implication, the peculiar metaphysical significance homosexuality had for Rimbaud. Because, doubtless, of its socially quite forbidden nature in the 19th century, homosexuality meant, potentially, an adventure into an unknown region of ethical and existential consequences. "Car il [le poète] arrive à l'*inconnu*," in the words of the second *lettre du voyant*. Verlaine seems to have shared this view with Rimbaud for a while. However, by the time Verlaine wrote "Crimen Amoris," his thought shows the attitudes that led to his formal conversion not quite a year later.

"Crimen Amoris" represents the Feast of the Seven Sins, at which the most beautiful of the evil angels, sixteen years old, as Rimbaud was when Verlaine met him, is overcome by metaphysical torment and addresses the saints and fallen angels:

> Vous le saviez, qu'il n'est point de différence
> Entre ce que vous dénommez Bien et Mal,
> Qu'au fond des deux vous n'avez que la souffrance,
> Je veux briser ce pacte trop anormal.
>
> Il ne faut plus de ce schisme abominable!
> Il ne faut plus d'enfer ni de paradis!
> Il faut que l'Amour, meure Dieu, meure le Diable!
> Il faut que le bonheur soit seul, je vous dis!

(You know that there is no difference between what you call Good and Evil, that in both of them you find only suffering. I want to break this abnormal pact. This abominable schism must be done away with; there must be no more hell or paradise! Even if God and the Devil both have to die, love and happiness alone must exist, I tell you!)

We see here a very striking characterization of Rimbaud's thought in 1872, which brings out certain things that are more implied than explicit in the poems which have been preserved: the rejection of original sin and God, the desire to abolish the suffering which weighs on life, and the central importance of *bonheur*, "happiness" or "beatitude." The notion of deification suggested by *bonheur*, in the sense of "beatitude," is made clear when the Rimbaud figure is depicted as saying he will create God himself, meaning presumably that he will attain the status of deity. Finally, he proposes to outdo Jesus, who merely maintained the balance of good and evil, by destroying hell in a vast conflagration as a sacrifice to Universal Love, recalling the lines: "Que le temps vienne / Où les cœurs s'éprennent" ("Chanson de la plus haute tour"). Verlaine's conclusion is that God, who still exists, does not accept the sacrifice and maintains the existence of evil and that the evil angel destroys himself, one of the attitudes Verlaine was to take towards Rimbaud in the immediately following years, before time transformed the latter and Verlaine wrote his late poems on his "grand péché radieux."

After this striking attempt to render the theological drama of Rimbaud's mind, which is presented with a kind of sharpness characteristic of Rimbaud, even though Verlaine meant to be more hostile and negative, Verlaine wrote "Du fond du grabat," a poem which covers, in symbolic fashion, the period of his association with Rimbaud, his "tenace démon." The ending anticipates Verlaine's conversion, and, while the poem is a bit uneven, it is fascinating to read in conjunction with *Une Saison en enfer* for the images that occur in both works, yet are different in significance and handling.

VII

Rimbaud's sense of failure was, at some point in late 1872 or early 1873, illuminated by a theological realization which is developed in the opening sections of *Une Saison en enfer* and which gave a sense of pattern to his own life, so that *Une Saison* is at once a very tightly and intricately constructed poem and a somewhat stylized autobiography.

The discovery Rimbaud made was that of historical determinism, which is explored in the complicated twistings and reversals of "Mauvais Sang," where the hypothesis of his being a true pagan and free of Christian original sin are developed with their antitheses and situate the poet, at the end, clearly in France and in the late 19th century. The significance of these hypotheses is implicit, as suits the elliptical style, but with "Nuit de l'enfer," the second section, originally entitled "Fausse Conversion," we arrive at the basic discovery that the poet's fate and sensibility have been determined by his baptism, seen as one of those rituals which are actually metaphysical events. As a result, his spiritual aspirations, however free they may seem from Christian ideas like those of God and original sin, are actually a disguised form of Christian thought, which in the end reveals the sinister dualisms of orthodoxy.

The separation of body and spirit, which represents a major aspect of the dualism of good and evil, had been perceptible in all the poet's aspirations towards a discarnate ascent into light. The desire for the good in Christianity always turns into evil, the two being inseparable and connected in an endless dialectic of reversibility. Evil is not, for the baptized, a subsidiary, contingent aspect of life: the plaintiveness, misfortune and suffering of the poems of 1872 culminated in the threat of metaphysical death, which stands opposed to salvation. Christianity is, moreover, paradoxical and insidious: asceticism, which is part of its traditions, is actually self-mutilation and grounds for damnation as a defacement of the work of God. Thus, the conversion to a kind of *bonheur,* ostensibly free of God and original sin, represents a demonic illusion, symbolized by the high summer light of the season in hell.

In the drafts and in the final texts of "Nuit de l'enfer" and "Alchimie du verbe," Rimbaud characterizes his "musiques naïves" of 1872 as "spells" or "magies religieuses," poems designed to provoke the illusions of the *dérèglement des sens.* "Je hais maintenant les élans mystiques": Rimbaud indicates quite clearly the influence the mystic tradition had had upon him. He also makes clear that mysticism is a false form of deification: at the height of his spiritual aspirations, as they are represented in "Nuit de l'enfer," the poet sees himself as Christ surrounded by the fires of hell. The whole section, interestingly enough, is dominated by the imagery of drinking poison (a version of the draught sought in "Comédie de la soif" and elsewhere), which provokes burning, dessication, and discarnation, all demonic variations on the mystical ascent of "Fêtes de la patience."

The two sections entitled "Délires" deal with the poet's exterior changes of mood from fury to sympathy and with his inner life, the latter represented by the spiritual exercises constituted by the poems of 1872. In "Alchimie du verbe," these are arranged in a cycle with a commentary on the feeling of bodily dissolution their creation brought on. The word *bonheur* emerges at the end, as "O saisons" is used, in a slightly modified form, to evoke the poet's heretical aspirations on Easter eve and his final realization of being damned through excess of spiritual aspiration. The last line ("Cela s'est passé. Je sais aujourd'hui saluer la beauté") closes the cycle begun when he cursed beauty in the violence of his revolutionary fury and hatred of society.

The comments in "Nuit de l'enfer" on the poems of 1872 as "spells," *magies religieuses,* are balanced by the ironic description, in "Alchimie du verbe," of the poet's work of that time as a "hallucination of words." The *dérèglement de tous les sens* is summed up by this derisive explanation; the "plenitude of the great dream" is seen as a linguistic suggestion. Rimbaud had tended to see poetry in terms of ideology, or in this case, theology, rather than as a problem in the behavior of otherwise normal words. This tendency led to his investing words with an otherworldly power and existence, in keeping with the dualisms of both the second *lettre du voyant* and the spiritual quest of 1872. When the poet sees language in and for itself in "Alchimie du verbe," he devalues his poems of 1872 as corresponding to no reality. These constitute the last direct remarks on language in Rimbaud's œuvre, but, as we shall see, there are interesting implications about it in the *Illuminations.*

It is important to understand the process of demystification represented by the sections of *Une Saison* which conclude with "Alchimie du verbe." By this I refer not only to the rejection of spells and mysticism, but also to the general sense in which Christianity is a mystery, with its paradoxes of good and evil. Blake, who abhorred the specters of dualism, represents Christ as crucified on the "tree of Mystery," which is, of course, that of the knowledge of good and evil. Rimbaud scarcely ever uses the word "mystery," unlike many 19th-century French writers who found mystery enchanting, but one senses that mystery, in the theological sense of something beyond the reach of reason, lies behind his whole representation of the season in hell. His long prose poem, however, is a way of combatting the Word with the Word: by writing it, he exorcises the specters of original sin and baptism, preparing himself for the new venture in poetic epistemology which the *Illuminations* will constitute.

Various propositions derived from 19th-century currents of thought are explored in the three short sections which follow "Alchimie du verbe," and finally, in "Adieu," a brief summation of the poet's life is made, concluding: "J'ai cru acquérir des pouvoirs surnaturels." He is left with a "devoir à chercher," his usual commitment to work and duty, and the continued pursuit of "la clarté divine" in the true sense, after the otherworldly delusions of the summer of "Alchimie du verbe." With the phrase "l'heure nouvelle," one of the most important adjectives of the *Illuminations* suddenly obtrudes, and it is followed shortly by the famous line, "Il faut être absolument moderne." One of the meanings of these words is obvious, if we contrast them with the *vieillerie poétique* the poet had turned to in his season in hell, the naïve mystic rimes, the poem conceived of as a spell, the creation of a stylized pastoral. The idea of modernism, strong in the *lettres du voyant*, returns, but modified in sense by the poet's passage through the season in hell. The imagery of "spiritual combat"—an old expression from 17th-century religious exercises—takes concrete form: the poet has fought beyond the "horrible shrub," the tree of knowledge of good and evil, symbolizing Christianity. This is the poet's night vigil before entering, at dawn, the apocalyptic "splendid cities." The exact connotations of all this remain slightly ambiguous up to the last line: there is a certain inevitable coincidence of Rimbaud's imagery of warfare and taking the city with Christian traditions of symbolism, but the images are free of any exact Christian and otherworldly reference, as is made clear by the final line: "et il me sera loisible de *posséder la vérité dans une âme et un corps.*" The separation of body and soul or spirit, which French Romantic social thinkers always reproached Christianity with, is at an end; its deleterious effects have been explored in the whole season in hell section, where spirituality leads to death. Curiously enough, Rimbaud's words reflect his reading of the texts of the New Testament which predate the full development of Christian theology: "therefore glorify God in your body and in your spirit" (I Corinthians 6:20); "there is one body and one spirit" (Ephesians 4:4). There was a project Rimbaud undertook, but did not finish, near the time of the writing of *Une Saison en enfer* (some fragments appear on the back of drafts for *Une Saison*), which was a retelling, as it appears, of the Gospel of Saint John. We know nothing of his intentions really, but the very fact that Rimbaud had pondered the subject enough to begin writing indicates the profoundly theological character of his imagination.

In its most general sense, *Une Saison en enfer* can be described as a cycle beginning with the classic forms of Romantic alienation—from self, from society, from beauty, as it is understood, from God—and concluding with reintegration and the achievement of wholeness. Like many Romantic cyclic patterns, it is analogous to the Christian and Neoplatonic ones of division, fall, and the achievement of a higher form of the original state of unity. Accidents of death, mental illness, and failure of poetic powers did not always permit such poetic designs to reach completion—one thinks immediately of Hugo's triptych of *La Légende des siècles, La Fin de Satan,* and *Dieu,* of the fragmentary state of Hölderlin's last poems, or of Wordsworth's projected plan for his last work.[13] Rimbaud, however, not only completed *Une Saison en enfer,* but went on to create another cycle of poems distinctly different in character.

Chapter III

ILLUMINATIONS

The composition of the *Illuminations* is now generally considered to be contemporary with and posterior to that of *Une Saison en enfer.* For reasons I shall shortly expose, I do not think that it matters exactly when the first ones were written. The "first ones," however, cannot be identified; part of the problem in reading the poems is that they were arranged and published in an arbitrary order by the first editor. The abundance of verbal and thematic parallels and echoes in them seems to demand some ideal arrangement, that is, one corresponding to a general idea such as Rimbaud must have had, at some level of exactness of articulation and consciousness, by the time he finished them. I shall present them in such an ideal fashion, but their looseness or tightness as a group, the irrelevance of the date of composition of the individual poems, and the manner in which they came to form a group suggest an excursus on genetic questions in Romantic and modern literature. It is for lack of understanding such general problems that critics of the *Illuminations* often fail in their readings of the poems. A "retrait du signifié" tends to occur more frequently on the part of readers than on that of Rimbaud.

It is common for modern poets to work in more than one style at a time and to use contrasting or seemingly contradictory thematic material, as Mallarmé does in "A la nue" and *Un Coup de dés.* The end of the work of art may be conceived of and executed before the beginning, or its true form and significance may change or actually emerge only when its composition is well under way. Proust pointed to *La Comédie humaine* and *Der Ring des Nibelungen* as works whose authors did not initially conceive of the form they were to invent, and Proust's own novel is another work that changed totally when he was over a third of the way into his original plan. The first and second editions of *Les Fleurs du mal*, whose significance was completely altered by the addition of a few poems of a new theological cast, is a nice example of the modification of existing poems by their juxtaposition with others, and such may well have been the case of the *Illumina-*

tions. Sometimes the artist may not have any clear notion of where he is headed as he begins a work: the *Duineser Elegien* seem to have baffled Rilke for years, as he worked at them on and off, and it is difficult to assess Pound's intentions throughout the earlier *Cantos.* Transposition of parts may be possible as well, without damaging the work, as study of the genesis and composition of "Le Cimetière marin" shows. I think all these problems of tentativeness, indirection, and the clear emergence of a theme after the fact, so to speak, may have played a role in Rimbaud's elaboration of the *Illuminations.* Of course, the theme may appear different to writer and public, as did that of *The Wasteland,* whose author was less conscious of his historical theme than his readers and more aware of the psychological drama of his poem. Although sometimes the coherence of a work of art may continue to defy critics in what seems to be a permanent fashion, as is perhaps the case of the two parts of *Faust,* there are actually deep-lying tendencies in modern poetry which provide a key to very puzzling works: one is cyclical organization, which we first find in the creative theologies of Wordsworth, Novalis, Hölderlin, Hugo, and others and which becomes widespread in later long works; the second is the systematic use of irony, so that there appears initially to be a great deal of self-contradiction in the work, whose propositions do not have the neatness of an orderly exposition.

We are fortunate in having a great deal of information about Romantic and modern creative processes, and if one reflects seriously on the facts, tendencies, and principles I have just summarized, it becomes possible to imagine how Rimbaud's work grew. We shall find much in the *Illuminations* that shows the recurrence of Rimbaud's earlier preoccupations, such as Romantic social thought or the cyclic organization of individual and historical experience. At the same time, such material is modified by the brilliant diversity of styles, the increased use of symbolic modes, and the presence of ideas adumbrated in *Une Saison en enfer.*

Perhaps the best way actually to begin reading the *Illuminations* is to observe, with a precise example, the dualistic sensibility of which *Une Saison* is a record and a criticism. In "L'Eclair," the poet, having realized the futility of his hopeless dialectic of aspirations towards the divine and demonic, considers the possibilities of some philosophical escape, but, wearied, lapses into the old dualism:

Ma vie est usée. Allons! feignons, fainéantons, ô pitié! Et nous existerons en nous amusant, en rêvant amours monstres et univers fantastiques, en nous plaignant et en querellant les apparences du monde, saltimbanque, mendiant, artiste, bandit, —prêtre! Sur mon lit d'hôpital, l'odeur de l'encens m'est revenue si puissante; gardien des aromates sacrés, confesseur, martyr . . .

(My life is worn out. Come on, let's pretend, be idle, O pity! And we shall exist on amusing ourselves, dreaming of monstrous loves and fantastic universes, complaining and railing against the outward appearances of the world—a clown, beggar, artist, bandit, priest! On my hospital bed the odor of incense comes back to me so strong—keeper of the sacred aromatics, confessor, martyr!)

The brilliant use of a stream-of-consciousness technique, which character-izes much of *Une Saison en enfer*, permits us to see with especial clarity the complementary character of good and evil, the divine and the demonic. Thoughts of revolt and alienation are suddenly converted into a fantasy of sanctity. Dialectic reversal could not find a more striking stylistic expres-sion. The kind of feeling represented by this passage is what the poet of the *Illuminations* must renounce. He is trying to construct a new vision of life in which the dependence on otherworldly moral principles will no longer be a trap continuously limiting his actions to pursuits of good or evil in a received sense.

Rimbaud's subsequent comment on the preceding quotation is "Je reconnais là ma sale éducation d'enfance." The bitterness of tone expresses the poet's disgust at finding himself constantly imprisoned in a sensibility he inherited. In contrast, the tone of one of the *Illuminations*, "Dévotion," shows the point of view of one who has passed beyond dualism and can look back on it with some equanimity. The poet thinks over some of the same matters as in *Une Saison*: the religious élans of his "false conversion" and the touch of depravity which it seems to bring with it. He first lists the people to whom his act of devotion is directed: two Romantic-sounding Sisters of Charity (charity is a key word for delusive Christianity in *Une Saison*),[1] the "adolescent" he had been, an old holy man (perhaps the person he might have become), and Lulu, the demon, with whom are asso-ciated chapels and a volume of lesbian verses by Verlaine (*Les Amies*). The poet generalizes further, adding, in a form which is at once like a prayer and a leave-taking, "every place of worship" in which he could not resist acts of reverence because of his "peculiar vice" of distorted religiosity. Rimbaud's blend of pensiveness and irony is very different from his remark in *Une Saison* about "ma sale éducation d'enfance" because he is saying farewell, in a definitive psychological break, to holiness, God-stricken erot-omaniacs like Lulu and Verlaine, the figuratively shipwrecked, mentioned also in *Une Saison*, and the stinking summer grass, which, alluding to the second of the "Fêtes de la patience," symbolizes his mystical aspirations. "Dévotion" is a vigil, as at the end of *Une Saison*, before the dawn of a new state of being, in which body and spirit are one; "metaphysical trips" are rejected with all otherworldliness, and the concreteness and wholeness of self will be affirmed by "violent exploits."

The place of the poet's leave-taking is the "polar chaos," chaos being the state from which a new world arises and the pole part of the peculiar cosmological vision of the *Illuminations*: cold and height (we must, in this imaginative world, see the North Pole as elevated) represent strength and clarity of mind. Completing this new kind of cosmological symbolism is the mention of a strange proper name, "Circeto" (*Circe* blended with *Ceto*, a sea deity, suggesting *ketos*, "whale"; ambiguously a place name or the first of a mysterious series of female figures who are found in various *Illuminations*). As goddess, Circeto is associated with the poet's silent prayer for the future. Temporality, so essential to the cyclic movement of the *Illuminations*, is stressed by the last elliptic words: "But no more [worship and metaphysics] from now on." It is a characteristic movement of the cyclic pattern, furthermore, that after a passage of a certain intensity and solemnity even, like this act of devotion, there is a fading out or rejection of the emotion evoked. The poem looks two ways: countering the slightly nostalgic recollection of the emotional burden of Christian dualism is an anticipation of the future.

We might, employing a touch of the irony characteristic of the *Illuminations*, take "Matinée d'ivresse" as a morning following the vigil of "Dévotion": it is an exploratory evocation of the new psychological state beyond the metaphysics of good and evil. The combat imagery of the end of *Une Saison* and the "violent bravura" or heroism of "Dévotion" are present, but the revolutionary violence is internalized. The poet is no longer alone, as in those poems, but his companion is a shadowy second self in the homosexual eroticism which is the theme underlying the poem's intricate imagery.

Homosexuality does not lie at the end of the poet's quest in the *Illuminations*, but it serves, in this first stage of stock-taking, to represent at once the passage beyond good and evil and the affirmation of the body: "*my* version of the good, the true, and the beautiful," the poet says, a bit more elliptically, in one of those allusions characteristic of the poem. The famous tripartite ideal associated in 19th-century France with Victor Cousin, is replaced for the poet by another trio of excellences, "l'élégance, la science, la violence," which, we should note, are all associated with the physical world in the *Illuminations*, unlike Cousin's Platonic threesome. Elegance, in its developments, will usually suggest bodies; violence is often replaced by the term "strength" (*force*), and *science* does not lead to the otherworldly, as in the poems of 1872, but is connected with the changing of life and even the creation of material enjoyments.

In "Matinée d'ivresse," there is a peculiar persistence of the idea of asceticism and self-torment, connected with homosexuality. The rack and poison images show how violence is more self- than other-directed in the poem, and the allusion to the medieval Moslem sect of the Assassins in the last line must be seen in this light: there is a good deal of suggestion of acquiring strength through self-violence, attempts on one's own life, in the poem and merely a vague horror of the outer world, with its oriental slaves.

The abundant religious reference of "Matinée d'ivresse" runs from calling orgasm "eternity," in what seems to be a parodic ritual sexual act accompanied by cultic incense, to the hymnic phraseology of the penultimate paragraph, in which we perceive an ironic Biblical pastiche, typified by the use of the very scriptural verb "glorify." The "method" celebrated by the poem alludes to the use of that term in philosophy ("the means for arriving at truth") or in devotional literature, where it is the equivalent of "spiritual exercise." Œuvre, like some other polyvalent words and concepts of "Matinée d'ivresse," has, among its connotations, certain religious ones, as in l'œuvre de Dieu, bonne œuvre, œuvre de chair. We shall see how Rimbaud's very deliberate use of such a word will permit a change of mode in the poet's quest, as terms are modified in sense.

The negative and positive aspects of this achievement of "pure love" are presented in terms of cyclic irony, the sense that all will change and return to its old state, "our former disharmony." The movement towards the future at the end of the poem ("Voici le temps des ASSASSINS") is qualified not only by the suggestion of self-destruction, but by the insertion of the word "assassin" into the whole stream of parodic sacral or oriental terms, of which the Biblical pastiche is doubly a part. In a sense, the whole poem suggests more an inversion of values than the creation of new ones, and this negative side of "Matinée d'ivresse" will make it an important point of reference with regard to other Illuminations.

The I of the Illuminations appears in different guises, anticipating the shifting voices of The Wasteland or The Cantos. With "Ouvriers," written with the plain, understated style of much fine realist fiction and contrasting strikingly with the elaborate poetic devices of "Matinée d'ivresse," we find the speaker again with a companion, this time his wife, or more likely his woman, Henrika, on the outskirts of a northern industrial city, whose mechanized looms send smoke far out into the wintry countryside. At first the focus is on Henrika's clothes, old and conspicuously inelegant. She is called "une chère image," a variation on the expression une belle image, a woman whose face lacks all expression. In this poem of negatives, there are allusions to negative progress (the industrial revolution), negative work (that of the mills), a kind of negative marriage ("nous ne serons jamais que des orphelins fiancés"; the word amour is absent), negative growth (the land smells of rot): in short, the unilluminated world, the desecrated or désacralisé land which is the opposite of the splendid cities glimpsed at the end of Une Saison.

The speaker, however, suddenly feels revolt:

O l'autre monde, l'habitation bénie par le ciel et les ombrages! Le Sud me rappelait les misérables incidents de mon enfance, mes désespoirs d'été, l'horrible quantité de force et de science que le sort a toujours éloigné de moi. Non! nous ne passerons pas l'été dans cet avare pays . . .

(Oh, the other world, the blessed abode of sky and shade! The South Wind brought back to me the wretched events of my childhood, my summertime despair, and the horrible amount of strength and knowledge fate has always kept from me. No! we will not spend the summer in this niggardly country.)

Here we see a modulation into the vocabulary of "Matinée d'ivresse": the speech itself is a form of violence, reinforced by the unstated determination to achieve strength and *science* and no longer to drag along, on his hardened arm, in a perpetually negative union, his "chère image." This is an allusion to the failure of heterosexuality as we see it, for example, in "Mémoire," and which will eventually be replaced by new relations between men and women.

But before the changing of life, the narrator broods on the fate devolved on him and the place of the past injustices which led to his present predicament. Essentially, this other world of the South is, before being the scene of injustice, the paradise of childhood, symbolizing mankind's primitive estate in the sun. Rimbaud makes use of this myth for its cyclical force— the poem makes us very conscious of both past and future at once—and because it is a natural part of para-Christian revolutionary myths, like the one he had early elaborated in "Soleil et chair."

In a related poem, "Ville," the speaker appears as a mindlessly content follower of a negative existence which resembles that of all his fellow citizens, who are, like him, "ephemeral"—the word suggests an insect in French and recalls the image, in *Une Saison,* of "les gens qui meurent sur les saisons," unlike the poet seeking divine radiance. The smoky city in "Ville" has no shadow of woods or summer night, like the South alluded to in "Ouvriers." Nor does it have "monuments of superstition," in the pretentious journalistic language of the speaker: it is beyond good and evil in a totally negative sense.

In this "metropolis" (a new word in the early 1870s, designating London), nothing interrupts the solitude of the like-seeming members of the populace except the appearance of the Furies, animating the muddy street in the figures of Crime, Hopeless Love, and Death. The presence of grotesque or evil female deities marks a couple of early *Illuminations,* where the regeneration of life has not yet taken place. There is a complex design of sexual reference in the *Illuminations,* which we shall see gradually unfold.

In one of the most strongly articulational of the *Illuminations,* "Jeunesse," we pass from images of the unilluminated world to those of the

changing of life. "Jeunesse" is one of the longest *Illuminations* and is written, especially in the first two of its four parts, in an extremely elliptical
style, in which, although many sentences are fairly long and grammatically
well developed, the relations of the words to each other are often hard to
seize. Nevertheless, we readily identify the key terms, which, to judge from
the drafts of *Une Saison*, were the initial elements by which Rimbaud sometimes plotted his prose, only later to work out the sentence structure. The
larger movement of "Jeunesse" is not at all unclear: it is structured as a
reflective poem, with autobiographical excursions into the past.

The "Hopeless Love" of "Ville" recurs in the opening images in the form
of a woman moaning over the improbable way she has been abandoned, a
sign of the disorders of heterosexuality; the smoke and fog characteristic
of the unilluminated world is referred to as the "carbonic plague." The
poet, however, sits alone in his room on Sunday and devotes himself to his
œuvre, which here has the sense of "work," in the large ambiguous range
of meaning going from the general idea of *travail* to the specific tasks of
the artist and builder. The *œuvre* is somehow connected with the "masses,"
and its means are mathematical and musical: the relevant terms are *calculs*,
rythmes, and, at the end of Part II, *voix* and *danse*. The musical images
are, in the *Illuminations*, a new part of Rimbaud's symbolism, and, just as
œuvre changes from ecclesiastical to constructional senses in "Jeunesse,"
so the blaring fanfares of "Matinée d'ivresse" are metamorphosed into
a highly intellectual music, perhaps even an unheard, theoretical one,
for which the association with mathematics is appropriate. The "masses"
of Part I undergo a transformation within the poem into the "humanité
fraternelle" of Part II: mankind is being formed and reconstructed into
a cohesive society. Part II also contains the word *force*: the evolution of
the poet's strength from the goal of "violent exploits" in "Dévotion" to
creative force is completed, and the latter is associated with right or *droit*.
(Most of these images are brought together, in similar fashion, in the brief
Illumination "Guerre.")

The poet's undertaking of his *œuvre* is a firm resolve, but doubts
and recollections of the past assail him in the beginning of Part II and in
Part III, where suggestions of crime, mourning, and eroticism bring to
mind the violent emotional climate of *Une Saison en enfer* and its "bri-
gands, les amis de la mort, les arriérés." The title of Part II, "Sonnet," and
the specific image of fruit hanging in the orchard allude to Verlaine's sonnet "Luxures," contemporary with *Une Saison* and filled with homoerotic
and theological concerns, all presented in a turbulent lyrical style.

"You are still at the stage of Saint Anthony's visions," states the poet,
in self-address, at the beginning of Part IV. This reference to the aberrantly

erotico-religious temptations of Saint Anthony of the Desert succinctly characterizes the "false conversion" described in *Une Saison,* the kind of sensibility represented by Verlaine's "Luxures," and the death-bearing dualism of Christianity. But then the poet confidently affirms the nature of his *œuvre,* which is the creation of a new world, in terms which have analogies with dominant modes of Romantic thought. The "harmonic" nature of the new world has different implications from the preceding musical images: while dance and singing are symbols of creation and order, as in a number of important poems from Wordsworth's "Solitary Reaper" to Wallace Stevens' "Idea of Order in Key West," harmony has, since the Pythagoreans, evoked the notion of a mathematically coherent universe; harmony is a complex system in a way the more linear singing and dance are not. The "architectural" nature of the new world, although less common in Romantic thought than harmonic structure, corresponds to the idea of the visual arts as purely formal and archetypical; it is significant that one of the most crucial instances of modernist controversy was to be architecture, because of its greater relation to life than that of other arts. Architecture is especially suitable for symbolizing the transformation of human existence. The "perfect" new bodies that will arise are much more a Romantic article of faith—as in "Soleil et chair"—than a private biological fantasy. Charles Fourier's notion that men will grow a tail with an eye on the end of it is merely the most grotesque—and therefore the most famous—example of this theory of evolution. We should note that Rimbaud's implications about the new bodies are more pansexual than specific; the poet's movement away from homosexuality is already marked.

We have seen that violence has been transformed into creative strength in "Jeunesse." Elegance is suggested by the perfect beings, and the whole *œuvre* implies *science,* with a strongly intellectual and even scientific connotation. We should observe now that creation, with a highly concrete, material basis, has replaced any thought of a state like *bonheur* and otherworldliness as the poet's goal. Also gone are the religious parodies, the ritual of "Matinée d'ivresse." The poet's demiurgic creation also represents the idea of a new form of work, as opposed to that of the unilluminated world of "Ouvriers." Despite all these resolutions of previous tensions, however, one question remains: the objectivity of the new world.

The poet describes his creation as arising from personal, subjective sources, but asks, "As for the world, when you leave your room, what will have become of it?" The answer, "Nothing of its present appearances," is a nice example of the ironies, in the form of hyperboles or understatements, which continuously give the *Illuminations* a rather indirect quality. The exterior world we have previously seen as a symbolic horror (for the poet of "Matinée d'ivresse" and his companion, with their secret ritual) and as a historical one (the industrial city of the late 19th century). The poet does not propose to transform the world into a spiritual, transcendent realm as in the *dérèglement des sens* of the poems of 1872, but to achieve change by intellectual means which are at once a form of private mental content and objective, operative forces: mathematics, with its subsidiary domains of harmony and science, is the bridge between the inner and the outer. Mathematics and its attendant disciplines will translate an idealistic mental content into reality. In all this, one should note that for Rimbaud, at this point, nature no longer has any special existence or meaning, as it did in his earlier poetry. He is not, in this respect, the anti-Romantic innovator he is sometimes claimed to be, but is conforming rather to a special line of Romantic thought, whose chief representative is Blake, but which also includes the very different ideas of Hölderlin and Novalis, who no more than Blake shared the Wordsworthian view of Nature.

Forward movement and retrogression are balanced in "Matinée d'ivresse," but with "Jeunesse" the cycle advances notably, as new or transformed conceptual material is added to the *Illuminations*. Opposing forces, however, meet in "Angoisse," in which the calm stateliness of "Jeunesse" IV vanishes.

The transformation of life glimpsed in "Angoisse" is rich in what for us may seem to be incongruously juxtaposed mythical and materialistic terms, but which are very characteristic of a Romantic system of thought like that of the Saint-Simonians, the most widely influential group of French social thinkers of the earlier 19th century.[2] There are, on one side, references to man's primitive state of freedom, to the demon-god, that is, one beyond good and evil, which the youthful poet has become, and to poetic symbols of peace, wealth, and perfection: palms and diamonds. The expression "féerie scientifique" combines in its two terms the mythical and materialistic. The latter side of Rimbaud's vocabulary is illustrated by worldly or economical terms: "ambition," "success," "wealthy old age." The Saint-Simonians joined a faith in applied science, in the reorganization of the work force, in material wealth, and in industrial production to notions of brotherhood (Rimbaud's "fraternité sociale"), the emancipation of women, the structuring of an ideal social order (the *œuvre*, in part, of "Jeunesse"), the reconciliation of body and spirit in a "New Christianity," and sexual freedom (represented by the poet's exclamation "Amour, force!"). One easily sees how, without even moving beyond the ambit of the Saint-Simonians, Rimbaud's Romantic social thinking can be traced to origins.

The enthusiastic central vision of the poet, in whom abound strength and *science*, in both senses, is countered by his feelings of actual failure, incapacity, and poverty. Framing the poem are two references which belong to an important chain of image-ideas in the *Illuminations*. At the beginning the poet wonders whether "She" will resolve his mental turmoil. This obviously favorable feminine power is contrasted with "la Vampire" (a word normally masculine) at the end of the poem, a creature who condemns the poet to inactivity and failure. We have seen the Furies appear in "Ville" and, in contrast, a kind of tutelary figure in the Circeto of "Dévotion." These are not supernatural powers, I believe, but symbols of parts of the mind, for it is not unusual that a man's mind is personified in part as feminine: the phrase "la force de Psyché" in "Jeunesse" II illustrates this, without our having recourse to Jungian exegesis. *Psyche, mens,* and *anima* are all feminine, and Rimbaud was a good enough classicist to have absorbed the habit of thinking in terms of Greek and Latin genders.

"Angoisse" closes with a vision of self-torment and drowning in turbulent waters, which makes a significant contrast with the notion of ascension earlier in the poem and recalls the self-punishment of "Matinée d'ivresse." We begin to see by this point many elements of recurrence and variation in related *Illuminations*. One word absent from most of the previous *Illuminations,* but present in "Angoisse," is *amour.* Joined with the terms *jeunesse* and *force,* it gives the impression of physical elegance with erotic implications, but *amour,* like certain other terms in the *Illuminations,* is a hinge word, capable of suggesting two directions of thought, erotic love and love as a social bond. The word has the same ambiguity in Saint-Simonian theory. One *Illumination,* "A une raison," concerns, in part, what seems to be love in a social sense, a fuller development of the expressions "humanité fraternelle" in "Jeunesse" II and "fraternité" in "Angoisse."

The title "A une raison" may use the personified noun with indefinite article in the vaguely flippant sense of some one of various ideas which are becoming embodied. We may also, however, be dealing here with one of Rimbaud's latinisms: *ratio* is a frequent word in Lucretius' description of the world dominates this somewhat abstract allegory. The results of these of the forces of reason ("Jeunesse": *calculs*; "Guerre": *logique*) organizing the world dominate this somewhat abstract allegory. The results of these forces are those found in "Jeunesse" IV: the creation of *new* men and a *new* harmony. *New* love is added, with further insistence on this important adjective in these *Illuminations*. Children cry for time to be abolished, that is, for cyclic variations in life to end. The expression "en-marche," applied to new men, suggests an undeviating forward progress to the end of time. The children also ask, in a Saint-Simonian-sounding note, for their material fortunes to be raised and their wishes—the basic rational wishes of new man —to be realized.

Some of Rimbaud's curious spatialism, in this case the temporal-spatial interrelation, is suggested in the final line, which seems, in its terse lack of a main verb, to be an ironic comment, perhaps balancing the oddity of the title of the poem: "Arrivée de toujours, qui t'en iras partout" ("Always arriving, you will go all over"). Here the irony seems to be of a general kind applicable to any hope of the ideal incarnating itself, as well as the cyclic irony of the notion that things always come and go. As is so often the case, this *Illumination* concludes with a temporal allusion.

The children who cry out in "A une raison" are not the only ones in the *Illuminations*. In "Matinée d'ivresse," in "Guerre," and in "Jeunesse" I, as earlier in "Mémoire," there are these enigmatic figures, often merely present at acts of great significance. They seem to represent mankind in innocent form contemplating the rises and reverses of fortune of the race. They are reminders of what Rimbaud calls "la franchise première," the primordial simplicity and freedom of man, and thus make one aware of the cyclic movement away from such a state. We shall find more children much later in the *Illuminations*.

The increasing concern with mankind as a whole, which we see in "A une raison," receives further development in "Soir historique," but here, instead of personifications and a kind of formal allegorical procession, we find a comic travel prospectus, a Thomas Cook and Sons treatment of the changing of life: "On whatever evening, for example, the naïve tourist finds himself in retreat from our economic horrors, the hand of a master brings to life the harpsichord of the meadows; there is a game of cards going on in the depths of the pond, a mirror summoning up queens and favorites. There are saints, veils, and threads of harmony." The references to the new illuminated world are contrasted with the fog we have seen in "Ville" and "Ouvriers": "The most elementary physicist feels that we can no longer put up with this personal atmosphere, a miasmal fog of physical remorse, the awareness of which is already an affliction." Rimbaud's symbolism of weather and climate becomes clearer: the "personal" atmosphere of the foggy city reminds us that in "Ville" no one speaks to anyone else; the maladjustments of contemporary heterosexuality ("les couples menteurs" and "l'enfer des femmes" of the end of *Une Saison*) seem alluded to by "physical" remorse.

The description of travel in "Soir historique" illustrates what might be called the use of seed phrases in the *Illuminations*. In "Jeunesse" IV the poet refers to his recreation of idle luxury and ancient crowds, which we find developed, in "Soir historique," into the images of queens, saints, revolts in the Celestial Empire, illuminated deserts in Tartary, moons, ballets, and so forth. Often a few words in one *Illumination* become a major subject of another. The principle of this imagery in "Soir historique" is continuous expansion of both time and space, the uninterrupted unfolding of our imaginative perceptions. Rimbaud ironically refers to this as "magie bourgeoise" or "home-style magic"—a phrase fabricated on the model of *cuisine bourgeoise*. We must not take "magic" literally, however, since the supernatural, as Rimbaud had associated it with his poems of 1872, has no place in this phase of the *Illuminations*.

The "idle luxury" of these spectacles of travel in time and space illustrates a kind of elegance. The "magie bourgeoise" is reinforced by references to *science* in its more modern senses: physics, geology, and finally cosmology, for the poem ends with "the time for the cosmological steam-bath, the removal of oceans, underground conflagrations, the planet off its course, and the consequent exterminations—certainties so unsubtly indicated in the Bible and by the Norns." Rimbaud alludes to the hypothesis of astronomical cataclysms in which mingle contemporary science and science fiction, just beginning in the 19th century. Time and space expand in the poem to the point of explosion. The irony of the last sentence of the "Soir historique" is apparent, even if its sense is not immediately clear, as is so often the case in the *Illuminations*: "But it won't be an effect of legend!" The important implication here is that the travels in time and space or cosmic upheaval are not otherworldly delusions or transcendent experiences, but take place on the plane of real life. Legends, Bibles, and Norns have nothing to do with these scientific realizations or predictions. We may, of course, read the travel imagery as a symbol of the imagination, even though that concept, as such, is not to be found in Rimbaud in any developed form. We must, however, in that case remember Blake's contention that the imagination is not transcendent: there is no other world.

The idea of the free perception of time and space is fundamental to the first phases of the cycle of the *Illuminations*. Rimbaud draws on quite varied cosmological concepts in his poems, ranging from the more or less scientific one of "Soir historique" to the naïve, but imaginatively satisfying conception of the North Pole as a high place, as in "Dévotion," in which we see both a relic of the old imagery of transcendence (Mount Sinai, Olympus) and the Alpine sublime of more recent literature. It is notable that, in keeping with the absence of a particular concept of nature, the elements of landscape tend to be unstable, symbolic, metaphorically inorganic, or otherwise to diminish the feeling of stasis and contact with the natural. The occasional exceptions will deserve a special kind of commentary.

The use of pronouns, as it varies among *Illuminations*, is most significant. Initially, in "Dévotion," the poet was alone; with "Matinée d'ivresse" he had a sexual partner of no special identity; the speaker of "Ouvriers" has only a doll-like woman as mate; in "Ville" solitude is emphasized. Creation occupies the isolated poet of "Jeunesse." In "Angoisse," alone still, the last first-person speaker of this series is found, in which the only variation is the self-address in the second person of "Jeunesse." The second-person address of "A une raison" involves an expanding perspective and relation to the world, as does the pronoun reference of "Soir historique," where the speaker passes from "our" economic horrors to a generalized third person representing men as a whole. It is only with "Génie" that the speaker becomes absorbed in the crowd of men, for here the relationship depicted is that between us and the *génie*, and the pronouns are *nous* and *il*.

Attributes are heaped on the *génie* which recall previous poems: he is affection, present, future, *force*, a "raison merveilleuse et imprévue," eternity, and love. This last term is developed fully now: the *génie* represents a musical love, "l'amour réinventé," in which inequalities like women's anger and men's gaiety will vanish, for they belong to the old bodies, the outworn form of the couple or *ménage*. "L'amour est à réinventer," says the *époux infernal* in *Une Saison*, and "Génie" marks the moment in history when this takes place. There is even a suggestion that mankind's relation with the *génie* has an erotic dimension: "We have all had the terror of his yielding and our own: oh joy in our health . . . and passion for him, who loves us for his infinite life." Reciprocity and mutual involvement characterize the *génie* and mankind in their emotive life. There is a rising pattern of meanings of love in the *Illuminations*: from homosexuality in "Matinée d'ivresse" and "Hopeless Love" in "Ville" through the pansexuality of "Jeunesse" and love of mankind in "A une raison" to the characterization of the most important relations in life as charged with erotic energy: the relation with the *génie* is the archetype of relations among mankind: "He has known us all and loved us all."

The new erotic dimension of life is correlated with the disappearance of Christianity: "Adoration" or "Worship" vanishes and "kneelings" are lifted; that is to say, the old relation of inferiority and disparity between man and deity has gone. The slave morality of Christianity depends also on the elaborate games God plays with Christ, who descends, rises, and promises a Second Coming. Out of this pattern Hölderlin drew the *tragique* of his poetry. But in the new era, redemption is now; the *génie* will never rise to heaven or descend. Redemption is enhanced existence, according to the influential Romantic theologian Schleiermacher, which shows the parallels with Rimbaud's thinking in actual religious philosophy.[3] The old inferior relation to God is replaced by an "affection égoïste" for the *génie*, and benevolent pride proves superior to the old charity, which is a key word for Christianity in *Une Saison*.

In "Matinée d'ivresse" we read: "on nous a promis d'enterrer dans l'ombre l'arbre du bien et du mal." This *on* now is revealed as the *génie*, whose attributes are the three excellences set forth in the earlier poem: "le brisement de la grâce croisée de violence nouvelle" and "la perfection des formes et de l'action" suggest elegance, as well as violence, conceived of now as intense energy, while *science* is alluded to in the expression "fécondité de l'esprit."

We must now consider in more detail what the imagery pertaining to the *génie* represents in philosophical or theological terms. The first crucial question is whether the existence of the *génie* implies any transcendence, and I think poetic and philosophical Romantic theology is a help. Blake's declarations are forthright: "Man is All Imagination. God is Man & exists in us and we in him." "The Eternal Body of Man is the Imagination, that is, God Himself."[4] Modern Blake studies tend to emphasize that imagination and vision are not, for him, otherworldly and mystical; indeed, Blake had a horror of the mysterious and inaccessible. Therefore, God is brought down, if one looks at it with the old image of transcendence, and is made a bond between men in their highest faculty. The interpenetration of God and man is the most characteristic spatial image of this new theology. It is most relevant now if we juxtapose to Blake's radical thought some of the notions of Schleiermacher, the most significant of the Kantian theologians in Germany. Kant had replaced transcendence by transcendentalism as part of his destruction of the old metaphysics, and in the newer concept, there is no implication of "rising over and beyond" life. Schleiermacher formulated the reciprocal relations or interpenetration of God and man in many ways, for he rejected the dualisms of good and evil, deity and mankind. At an early point he made the following expressions synonymous: universe (*Weltall*), the genius of humanity, the world spirit, eternal love, destiny, and deity. All kinds of old distinctions are conflated in this radical refusal of transcendence, and we note that Rimbaud's *génie* and Blake's "poetic genius of man" have their correspondence in Schleiermacher's genius of humanity. The image of the *Weltall*, of the universal process, is clearly identifiable in the picture of Rimbaud's *génie* circling the earth. As for destiny, the *génie* is called at one point "machine [the old poetic word for world] aimée des qualités fatales." When Schleiermacher affirms that "Self-intuition and intuition of the universe are reciprocal concepts," he might be defining the relation between the *Illuminations* "Jeunesse" and "Génie." The notion of us in God and God in us is also to be found in Schleiermacher, for whom ideas of mutuality, as opposed to the old worship of the transcendent, are natural. It is valuable to compare Blake and Schleiermacher's thought with Rimbaud's because they all belong to different traditions and came at the same solution to problems from different points of view. Blake and Rimbaud were ignorant of Kant's radical revision of the character of philosophical inquiry, and their Protestant and Catholic backgrounds were quite dissimilar.

If we read through Rimbaud's poem asking ourselves whether the *génie* is part of us (he is affection, love, and so forth) or we are part of him ("immensité de l'univers" is one qualification applied to him), we find that Rimbaud has created a very delicately ambiguous work, and we are inclined to resort to paradoxes, such as "he is and is not part of us." He is archetypal or ideal man in his elegance, science, and violence, but when he is called "le charme des lieux fuyants," the *génie* could be our state of mind, as we perceive such spots, or the quality such spots acquire from an agency outside us. Typically, we find ourselves falling back on references to psychological states of ambiguous origins. In this, Rimbaud's poem is in accord with modern discussions of transcendence, which totally abandon the distinction of the this-worldly and the otherworldly for non-spatialized psychological descriptions.[5] The metaphysical connotations have fallen away from the term. For this reason, the old ideas of pantheism and panentheism are totally unsatisfactory in talking of such conceptions as Blake's, Schleiermacher's, or Rimbaud's.

There is an important series of expressions in "Génie" of which I have postponed discussion and in which we can see, in a sense, the synthesis or solution of the paradox of reciprocity. A large number of words associate the *génie* not simply with the universe, but with the universal cyclic process: "souffles" or gusts of wind, a common cosmological symbol, "jour" or recurrent light, and "musique plus intense" or a more Dionysiac kind of sound than the stable Pythagorean "harmony" of earlier poems. Cyclicity is stressed by such phrases as "Et nous nous le rappelons et il voyage . . ." and "[he whom] nous voyons passer dans le ciel de tempête et dans les drapeaux d'extase." The storm and ecstasy of this last line represent the intensity of human experience, both pleasurable and terrifying; balancing the reinvention of love is "le chant clair des malheurs nouveaux." However, process absorbs pain ("l'abolition de toutes souffrances dans la musique plus intense"), since man's ills are only empirical and accidental, and thus Rimbaud's poem is filled with the energy and rapture which come from identifying oneself with the cosmic pattern.

The endpoint of Rimbaud's "Génie" is very similar to Nietzsche's conception of the eternal return, for both are based on the idea of finding a philosophy beyond good and evil, beyond all thought of reward or punishment. For Nietzsche, there was a kind of austere joy in the idea of the recurrence of all things, which made up for the vanished idea of God or transcendence. It is part of the effect of cycles within cycles, so peculiar to the *Illuminations*, that when we reach "Génie," the high point of the first phase of the *Illuminations*, we find simply a more generalized, more philosophical conception of cyclicity. But, insisting on the parallel with Nietzsche again, we see that the peculiar tone of Rimbaud's version of the eternal return is not that of passive acceptance, but one of rejoicing in the rigor and harshness of life, for which the compensation lies in perceiving the universal design, unobscured henceforth by Christianity and its moral fog. Once again, we can see how severely intellectual Rimbaud's poetic conceptions basically are.

The higher thematic seriousness of "Génie" excludes the practical Saint-Simonian ideas of the reorganization of society and the new kind of work. One word in the poem, however, is the seed of "Mouvement": great "migrations" are mentioned. This *Illumination*, like "A une raison," is an allegory involving forward horizontal movement. The boat of humanity, the "ark," is its main symbol, complemented by that of a young couple standing at the prow in "harmonic" ecstasy: this is the first precise image of male and female union we have encountered, and it corresponds to the Saint-Simonian idea of the reinvention of sexual relations through freedom on the part of both men and women. The couple are part of a heroic movement of conquerors, implying *force*: they themselves incarnate bodily elegance, and the content of the ship corresponds to *science*. Temporally, the couple represents the same moment in history we have seen in "Génie," which is here called the emergence from "ancienne sauvagerie" or barbarism.

There is technical and scientific vocabulary in the description of the ship, mention of sports and *confort*, two words connected with the new enjoyment of life in the later 19th century, but little mention of nature beyond animals and flowers, the former evidently to be improved by scientific breeding, the latter vaguely symbolic of beautiful objects, like the jewels mentioned with them. Rather, the emphasis is on practical science, on "nouveauté chimique" and "fortune chimique." It is worth pausing for a moment to recall how imperfectly some sciences were organized for much of the 19th century and how well their theoretical vagueness lent itself to mythopoeia. It was only in 1869 that the periodic system of the elements was communicated to the scientific world, and organic chemistry, the basis of modern practical chemistry, did not take shape until after 1870, with the increasing study of complex molecules. Such a fragmentary and free-wheeling science as chemistry, the one Rimbaud alludes to most often, encouraged speculative literary references and Saint-Simonian hopes.

Contrasting spatial effects are very characteristic of the *Illuminations*, and in the first poem called "Villes" ("Ce sont des villes") the splendid cities of the end of *Une Saison* are evoked in a profusion of vertical and horizontal linear indications. There is deliberate excess and the impossibility of a graphic rendering. Nature, except for sea and sky, is almost absent, and the plenitude is, in part, legendary or mythological. The ideas of the people, the joy of the new work, and the unheard-of music which are mentioned suggest, together with the allusive imagery, an apocalyptic version of the Saint-Simonian new life, which, in itself, was an advanced idea, but not beyond hopes of realization. For example, in the "Programme de la Commune" of April 19, 1871, we find reference to "l'épanouissement du travail affranchi de toutes les entraves, livré à toutes les énergies."[6] We must be careful not to think of 19th-century social thought as divorced from any actual effort made to realize it. It is equally impossible to think of certain *Illuminations* as either mimetic or uniquely products of a fantastic imagination.

We encounter in the set-off last line of "Villes" a temporal indication which is, at the same time, a suggestive comment on the mode of reality of certain more descriptive *Illuminations*:

> Quels bons bras, quelle belle heure me rendront cette région, d'où viennent mes sommeils et mes moindres mouvements?

> (What arms, what fine hour will give back to me this region, whence come my dreams and my slightest movements?)

Erotic energy contributes to the vision, as is suggested by "Génie," where the *génie*'s gifts are sensory, concrete, and even sensual. Since the vision governs the poet's slightest actions, it can be conceived of as on the same plane with such mental forces as obsessive thoughts or will, whose reality can hardly be doubted. There is nothing otherworldly about the faculties of the mind, unless one chooses to invest them with transcendent, metaphysical implications.

The *Illuminations* we have been examining begin with a vigil, which symbolizes the beginning of a new phase of life, as in feudal customs. The changing of life is only half realized in "Matinée d'ivresse," where daily practice of the "method" cannot be separated from a daily return to disharmony. That poem generally symbolizes a work of destruction quite as much as one of rebuilding. The content of "Matinée d'ivresse" is an inversion of conventional values, whereas in the course of the next few *Illuminations* the progressive elaboration of themes leads finally to an *Umwertung aller Werte*, the Nietzschean transvaluation of all values we see in "Génie." The poet puts metaphysics behind him in "Dévotion," and, although Rimbaud probably did not know much about the more important modern philosophers, the intellectual movement of his poems follows the rejection of metaphysics made by Kant and the development of a scheme of thought free of the transcendent, like the one Blake devised or the one Schleiermacher evolved under the conscious influence of the Kantian revision of philosophical inquiry. Accompanying this evolution is one from subjectivity to objectivity, most simply represented by the pronominal usage of the poems. The future will be materialist, according to the second *lettre du voyant*, and we find that a progressive realization of ideas of concrete reconstruction tends to confirm this notion in this first phase of the *Illuminations*. "Villes," however, again puts a certain distance between the poet's mental imagery and his surroundings; with this poem we close that part of the cycle of the *Illuminations* which is concerned with mankind.

II

There is a group of *Illuminations* of primarily visual interest which we can describe, for purposes of organization, as having their seeds in the details of the first "Villes." Their imagery includes the elaborate structures of the second "Villes" ("L'acropole"), "Promontoire," and "Ponts" and the representation of processions, festivities, and theater in "Ornières," "Fêtes d'hiver," "Scènes," and "Bottom." Although there is reference to groups of people in most of them, the speaker of these *Illuminations* is usually not involved with them, for they are part of an elaborate visual design and not men seen *sub specie humanitatis*. Their *théories* or *défilés*, *baccanales*, *tarentelles*, and other activities are not even characterized as being part of life transformed. We encounter a distinction between these poems and those of the first phase which can be traced back to a much earlier point in Rimbaud's work.

One of the most curious features of "Les Poètes de sept ans" and of "Le Bateau ivre" is the juxtaposition of an apocalyptic vision of mankind's future with the visual imagery of a solitary personal adventure. The latter may impress one by its utter strangeness, as in the second "Villes," or contain the elements of a distinctive new visual esthetic, as in "Ponts." England and particularly London seem to have contributed something to certain poems which it is difficult for us to perceive in present-day London, but which has a historical reality, as some very interesting research has shown.[7] Victorian overbuilding; such oddities, for the times, as elevated trains and a subway; the fantastic eclecticism of Victorian architecture; the sheer size of the city, which caused it to be called a "metropolis," the first generalized use of the word; the relative height of the buildings, emphasized by contemporary drawings and photographs; abundant and varied theatrical entertainment, including exotic importations; the presence of vast crowds; and the peculiar light caused by damp air and dull skies—all these features of the city differentiated it for contemporaries from Paris and contributed to the formation of a special taste for the urban, which we find in both Rimbaud and Verlaine.

The enlarged and involuted visual perceptions of a number of *Illuminations* owe something to a relative historical reality—the effect of London on a Frenchman with a pronounced interest in modernity—but they also are, in part, purely mental sights, for the mind is, in some ways, a greater and more powerful eye than our physical ones. Indeed, Rimbaud's visions generally include effects which are, strictly speaking, unrealizable in material terms, his medium being words and his esthetic postmimetic to an ample degree. Thus his fantastic London can be juxtaposed to a poem like "Mystique," a title meaning something like "vision," which is an allegorical picture of mankind's collective experiences, such as war and progress, hanging over an enchanting blue abyss.

A poem that would appear from its title, "Fleurs," to be descriptive, constantly eludes visualization:

D'un gradin d'or, —parmi les cordons de soie, les gazes grises, les velours verts et les disques de cristal qui noircissent comme du bronze au soleil, —je vois la digitale s'ouvrir sur un tapis de filigranes d'argent, d'yeux et de chevelures.

Des pièces d'or jaune semées sur l'agate, des piliers d'acajou supportant un dôme d'émeraudes, des bouquets de satin blanc et de fines verges de rubis entourant la rose d'eau.

(From a great golden step—amid silk cords, gray gauzes, green velvets, and crystal disks darkening like bronze in the sun—I see the foxglove open on a carpet of silver filigree, eyes, and hair. Gold coins scattered over agate, mahogany pillars supporting a dome of emeralds, white satin bouquets, and fine ruby rods surrounding the water rose.)

The metaphorical character of the poem is its point. There is little left of nature in this imagistic world created by the most typical syntactic figure of the *Illuminations*: the joining of two nouns by *de*—that is, genitive modifiers and metaphor in preference to the use of adjectives—which forms, in many ways, the basic unit of metaphoric language. As often, the verb is reduced to a minimal role, but the visual kinesis which verbs bring about elsewhere is compensated for by the flickering instability of this pseudo-description, which cannot be totally visualized, as it teases the sense of sight. While temporal dynamism is lacking in this phase of the *Illuminations*, the complexities of Rimbaud's playing with the visual prevent these poems from being in any way static. It is obvious that considerable thought must have gone into working out paradoxes for the eye as a method—one which clearly establishes the fact of language as an experience in itself, beyond all concern for mimesis.

We are dealing here with poems which have implied in them a theory of language as a semi-autonomous reality: the individual words designate things which are clear enough, but their aggregate is not. There is a certain tendency perhaps in Rimbaud's poetry of the spring and summer of 1871 towards the visually unrealizable, but such diction does not seem to be exploited in a highly conscious fashion before the *Illuminations*. Nothing in the *lettres du voyant* suggests such a style, and we have no late remarks of Rimbaud's concerning language, so we must assume the theory from the results. The transcendent and the mystical, in the technical sense, are no more implied here, I think, than they are in Blake's spatial imagery, which, coming from the mental eye, does not follow the rules of the physical eye, without, for that matter, being otherworldly.

Although "Promontoire" deals explicitly with a palace of Art, in which Victorian eclecticism reaches those heights where bourgeois pomposity and surrealism join forces, by and large the symbolic content is small in these *Illuminations* of the second phase of the cycle. There is farce in "Nocturne vulgaire," which seems to refer to getting drunk, and in "Bottom," in which we find an elaboration on the *féerie* of *A Midsummer Night's Dream*, but, by and large, the speaker of these poems is impersonal, untroubled, or virtually absent. We therefore recognize that with two or three *Illuminations* whose stylistic techniques are similar to the other visual ones, the presence of obviously symbolic material or the intense involvement of the speaker points towards yet another phase of Rimbaud's cycle. One of these poems is "Fairy," in which astronomical imagery (the "legends" or constellations, the "impassibles clartés" in the sky, and the presence of stellar "influence") joins with pastoral theatrical imagery (the song of the woodcutters' wives) to lead up to Hélène's dance, which we may take as an image of creation or as a symbol of cosmic design. Dance is a ritual, but in this poem the dancer's origins are dwelt on just enough so that we cannot take her as a simple metaphor, as Mallarmé claimed dancers to be. The fact that she is female suggests that she represents most specifically the mind as it realizes the nature of the universe and its pattern.

The psychological value of Hélène the Fairy is matched by "notre mère de beauté" in "Being Beauteous." Our Mother of Beauty, to whom the word "Vision" is applied, appears against snow, symbolic of mental elevation, and behind the approaching poet is an army shooting at the Being Beauteous. But this is not an impersonal vision of universal pattern like "Mystique": the poet flings himself at the vision in an attempted sexual union, while harsh military music, the opposite of Pythagorean harmony, blares in the "light" or mountainous air. From fleshly and wounded, the Mother of Beauty turns into crystal, an image related to the diamond of perfection elsewhere in the *Illuminations*. Perhaps the most important thing about the poem is its spatial character: the world is "far" behind the poet, who is at the end of a quest; he seeks isolation with the Being Beauteous.

The temporal character of "Being Beauteous" is also pronounced, as is that of "Fairy," in which Hélène's dance constitutes an explicitly unique

moment, in the strongest sense of the adjective. The idea of a creative hour
lived beyond the world and its violence recurs in "Métropolitain," where
the imagery of place is developed more fully. The title was borrowed from
the London subway, which was partly covered, partly open, and the poet's
quest leads him from the dark enclosing skies of the city and the battle,
symbolic of man's life in its more material phases, through an open walk
into a fantastic landscape of initiatory character, to sunny polar snows,
where he is definitively above and beyond the world. The sense of reality
is greatest in high, snowy places; and in the morning sun, with fantastic
black flags, deep red polar scents, and blue rays of light in the air, he strug-
gles with his *force*, creative, feminine, and personified. The shade of meaning of *force* is, of course, one we derive from its most positive uses in
earlier *Illuminations*, and thus the poems mutually support one another.
This imagery of creative energy shows most clearly the psychological character of the female figures in the *Illuminations*. Feminine images are not so
often airily transcendent as masculine ones; rather, as here and in the end
of "Dévotion" or in "Being Beauteous," they are strongly connected with
places: the "décor unique" of "Fairy."

The transfiguring experience of "Métropolitain," made so vivid by the
color imagery, is expressed by a verb in the *passé simple*, the only such
tense in the poem: thus the singular character of the action joins with the
sudden revelation of its pastness to give a strong effect of cyclical movement. We have by now entered into the third stage of the cycle of the
Illuminations, and the more characteristic imagery of it is less dense and
involuted than in preceding *Illuminations*. "Barbare" nicely transposes
some of the thematic material of "Métropolitain" into a less agitated stylistic mode.

"Barbare," whose title probably means a barbaric poem in the sense
Leconte de Lisle used the expression—that is, a poem whose beauty is
totally unclassical—contains references back to other poems: "Long after
the days and seasons and the creatures and countries" seems to refer collec-
tively to the varied images of strange worlds preceding, while "recovered
from the old fanfares of heroism . . . far from the old assassins" alludes
specifically to "Matinée d'ivresse." We have reached the farthest distance
along the cycle from violence, homosexuality, and music in its harsh mode.
Even though he still hears echoes of the violent erotic world left behind, the
poet can no longer participate in it, for such loves have been converted, as
in the making of artificial diamonds, from carbon to a glowing frozen fire:
"Embers raining in blasts of frost—sweetness—flames in the rain of diamond-
wind, cast by the terrestrial heart, eternally charred for us." Diamonds sym-
bolize lucidity and perfection. These references to what "Barbare" occurs

after place us in some free-floating time, almost in eternity: there is no main verb in the poem to tie it to any temporal point.[8]

We find the high point of Rimbaud's polar symbolism in this world of silky waters, cold flames, ice music, and arctic flowers, dominated by a pavilion or flag (the word *pavillon* is ambiguous) of bloody meat—the great barbaric touch. The use of repeated words and circular form suggests that it is not stasis which is being represented, but a gentle regular movement, in which one feature stands out: "the feminine voice reaching the depths of volcanoes and arctic caves." Here the female symbol, connected with places and depths rather than being aerial, assumes very much a divine form, and the contact of the poet with the goddess is immaterial and explicit. Wholeness of mind is the symbolic sense of heterosexual union for Rimbaud.

There is, of course, very little of nature in any representational sense in "Barbare." Rimbaud underscores this fact by remarking twice of the arctic flowers that "they do not exist." Their inexistence is literally true, but it also suggests ironically and by synecdoche that the existence of the poetic world can be questioned. There is always something paradoxical about the notion of timelessness in poetry that no longer embodies the old metaphysics. It has been said that irony may lie "in being conscious of the revelation by which the Absolute in a fleeting moment, (yet resembling eternity,) is at once realized and destroyed, and art is but the moment of its passing, the beautiful and fragile phenomenal manifestation which both expresses and abolishes the idea."[9] Rimbaud's use of the phrase "they do not exist" perfectly captures this shade of Romantic irony. It is the culmination of all the ironic turns and twists in the first two phases of the *Illuminations.* The absolute does and does not exist, depending on a slight change of perspective or mood.

Whereas the union of masculine and feminine principles, the poet and beauty, the poet and his creative mind, the poet and the divine-seeming voice which fulfills him with its sound, has been highly symbolic, Rimbaud in "Royauté" expresses this junction in terms of heterosexual marriage, insisting on the reality of the completion represented by the male and female united. It is very important for the understanding of later *Illuminations* to realize that Rimbaud's symbolism has real heterosexuality, understood in its reinvented form, as its basis. Then, on the symbolic level, marriage signifies wholeness of body and spirit, the human and the divine, freedom and destiny, and the other dichotomies Romantic thought sought to resolve. Unity in self, according to Schleiermacher, represents the unity of God, or the universe.[10]

In the detail of "Royauté," we see a reversal of the situation of the speaker and Henrika in "Ouvriers," who suffer from fate and denial of fulfillment. "Royauté" takes place after a trial has been sustained:

> Un beau matin, chez un peuple fort doux, un homme et une femme superbes criaient sur la place publique: "Mes amis, je veux qu'elle soit reine!" "Je veux être reine!" Elle riait et tremblait. Il parlait aux amis de révélation, d'épreuve terminée. Ils se pâmaient l'un contre l'autre.

> (One fine morning, in the country of a very gentle people, a superb man and woman were crying out in the public square. "My friends, I want her to be queen!" "I want to be queen!" She laughed and trembled. He spoke to friends of a revelation, of a trial terminated. They swooned against each other.)

The marriage is subtly conveyed in the expression "king and queen" of the second paragraph, which also has another important implication:

> En effet ils furent rois toute une matinée où les tentures carminées se relevèrent sur les maisons, et toute l'après-midi, où ils s'avancèrent du côté des jardins de palmes.

> (In fact they were king and queen for an entire morning, during which the crimson hangings were raised on the houses, and for the entire afternoon, during which they advanced towards the gardens of palm trees.)

The *passé simple* tense, after the vague imperfects of the first paragraph, thrusts the event back into the past, like the *passé simple* at the end of "Métropolitain." The verb tense is a form of cyclic irony in itself, for we see, opposed to the durative expressions "for an entire morning" and "for an entire afternoon," the essentially fleeting character of the day. In modest form, the contrastive temporal indications again represent the paradox of eternity and passing time, as we perceive such categories psychologically, with no reference to the old metaphysics. Transparency of style sharpens the opposition.

Nature again scarcely appears in "Royauté," for the palm trees are laden with the symbolism of peace and fruitfulness. In "Aube," however, we find a more detailed landscape, and the temptation at first sight to read it as an allegory of the poet and nature, in the ordinary sense, is strong:

> J'ai embrassé l'aube d'été.
> Rien ne bougeait encore au front des palais. L'eau était morte. Les camps d'ombres ne quittaient pas la route du bois. J'ai marché, réveillant les haleines vives et tièdes, et les pierreries regardèrent, et les ailes se levèrent sans bruit.
> La première entreprise fut, dans le sentier déjà empli de frais et blêmes éclats, une fleur qui me dit son nom.
> Je ris au wasserfall blond qui s'échevela à travers les sapins: à la cime argentée je reconnus la déesse.

> (I kissed the summer dawn. Nothing was stirring yet before the palaces. The water was still. Encampments of shadows did not rise from the forest road. I walked, awakening warm and living breaths, and sparkling stones gazed, and wings silently rose.

My first adventure, in the path already filled with cool, pale gleams, was a flower who told me her name. I laughed at the blond waterfall whose streaming hair rose through the pines: at the silver crest I recognized the goddess.)

Rimbaud's imagery has two dominant features: it is filled with details involving light, including subtle expressions, such as that concerning precious stones, whose glance is their gleaming; and light brings on life, the rendering of which ranges from giving a new sense to still or "dead" waters through a series of personifications: breezes, stones, flowers, and the waterfall. Rimbaud is deliberately creating a heightened sense of reality; the presence of precious stones, the silver crest of the waterfall, and, later, the marble wharves of the town, all these somewhat unnatural phenomena, along with the personifications, fit in with the apparition of a goddess, a visionary if not transcendent figure. We see in the poem not so much nature in the Wordsworthian sense, or a natural supernaturalism, but a clear perception of the cosmic cyclic force higher than the level of the organic: light is its manifestation.

The feminine nature of the visionary figure who symbolizes heightened consciousness permits an interesting transition from the sense of light to the corporeal seizing of the goddess. Masculine supernatural figures, especially those associated with light, tend to resist firm incarnation and to rise in an illusion of transcendence, whereas the feminine is more commonly associated with the earth:

En haut de la route, près d'un bois de lauriers, je l'ai entourée avec ses voiles amassés, et j'ai senti un peu son immense corps. L'aube et l'enfant tombèrent au bas du bois.
Au réveil il était midi.

(Where the road rises over a hill, by a laurel wood, I embraced her in her mass of veils, and I felt somewhat the shape of her immense body. Dawn and the child fell to the bottom of the wood. On wakening, it was noon.)

It is part of a highly unusual symbolic design to have a figure of light, one appearing at the crest of a waterfall, where the waters gleam most, become so heavy as to be able to fall, for it is the goddess whose weight drags the child after her. The brief last paragraph employs a word, "noon," which is regularly used in indicating clock time, whereas "dawn," of course, has no fixed location in the cycle of the hours: dawn is at once in and out of time, in the clock sense, and the ambiguity by which it is related to noon and yet has no exact hour permits the ironic fall from a high vision of the cosmic cyclical force to a dull perception of it as a limiting, constricting, wearisome repetitive pattern, as is implied in the final paragraph. The poem moves from the kind of intense, involving perception we find in "Génie" ("lui qui est le charme des lieux fuyants et le délice surhumain des stations") to the opposite impression of experience: the eternal return is not the source of an austere joy, but the dreary apprehension of clock time, which is circular in the most unfavorably symbolic sense. It is the connotations of the female figure, ranging from the symbol of the mind in its highest perceptual mode, through the sexual notion of fulfillment of self and the universe in perfect union, to the physical earth-bound nature of man with all his limitations, that allows "Aube" to constitute one of the most amazing turning points in the *Illuminations*.

III

We have observed distinctive uses of tenses in more than one *Illumination*, and the implications of remoteness in time of episodes of union with a female figure. A far more explicit temporal pattern in "Après le déluge" retrospectively clarifies earlier poems. In a cohesive syntactic frame, the poet tells how "as soon as the idea of the Flood had subsided," a new world came into being and that, "since then," spring arrived. The imagery of the new world has details recalling other *Illuminations* in which the emotive burden is, in part at least, quite positive: the flowers and precious stones of "Aube," the polar chaos of "Dévotion," the child of "Aube," the group of children of various *Illuminations*, and the detailed plenitude of activities of poems like "Soir historique" and the first "Villes" recur here. At the climax of this central section of "Après le déluge," a nymph, a kind of goddess, appears.

Suddenly, imperatives call for the floods to begin again, and the poet explains that the creation of a world was an "ennui." The irony is, however, that floods and creation are part of a natural cycle, just like that analogue of the circadian cycle by which delight and ennui alternate in men. Cosmic forces destroying or creating can do nothing more than follow a fated, repetitive movement. But unlike the poet of "Génie," the speaker of "Après le déluge" can take no pleasure in the world process, for he himself is enslaved by the psychological and biological cycle which dictates positive and negative feelings to him in turn. There is even a suggestion, in the opening expression "the idea of the Flood," that the poem is an allegory of fantasies and moods. The poet is, in any case, not one of the new men of the earlier *Illuminations*: no biological evolution, such as was envisaged in Romantic social thought, has transformed him into a creature of boundless energy and enjoyment of his condition.

The cycle of the *Illuminations* is now in its final, downward phase. The poet complains of the Queen, the Witch, who lights her embers in earthenware: the female figure has changed from the nymph Eucharis (the "gracious") to a hostile despot, associated with clay and destiny. Specifically, the poet regrets that she "will never consent to tell us what she knows, and we do not." *Science* is what is being withheld from him, as in "Ouvriers," early in the *Illuminations,* where fate decreed his weakness and ignorance. Significantly, he envisages *science* in the form of magic, the kind of knowledge a witch has. Magic has the implications of self-deception it came to have in *Une Saison,* where the poet's false conversion is seen as a delusion of magic powers. One senses on what a different plane the *magie bourgeoise* of "Soir historique" is played out. There is legitimate knowledge, mathematics and harmony, and the false knowledge of magic, which appeals to those suffering from ennui and alienation desiring immediate contact with some unknown absolute.

Secret knowledge is a characteristic theme of the declining phase of the *Illuminations* which is thus related to "Matinée d'ivresse" at the beginning of the cycle and opposed to collective notions such as "the ideas of the people" in the first "Villes." "H" is written in the form of an enigma, although it is not difficult to see that Hortense represents sexuality and body divorced from mind or idea, in contrast to Hélène the "Fairy," who stands for the mind tranquilly perceiving cosmic patterns. Instead of the unique hour of "Fairy," Hortense is associated with the long, cruel, barbarous history of man, whose "hygiene" or outlet she has been, even for the poorest. The suggestions of masturbation and prostitution in the poem merge in a kind of pansexual effect. The enigmatic children, associated with mankind's origins, are present, and history, seen as dependence on sexuality, is characterized by "monstruosités." Hortense's gestures are horrible; she is mechanical and violent, destroying the decadent men of today: this is a poem of unilluminated mankind. The last line summons up her consuming horror: "Oh terrible shudder of erotic initiations on the bloody ground and in the hydrogenic glare!"

The curious effect of inversion in regard to an earlier *Illumination* is illustrated nicely by "Parade," a number of the themes of which can be seen as constituting an antithetical reference to "Soir historique." In the earlier poem, the ordinary middle-class citizen, for a kind of theatrical entertainment, traveled to distant times and places by *magie bourgeoise* or science. The poem's imagery is characterized by the effect of expansion, as geographical and astronomical references become more remote and fantastic. In "Parade," on the other hand, the ordinary citizen stays at home, and players come to town who have something of the air of an invading force: "Very tough types. Several have exploited your worlds."

Their contempt for the citizen is expressed by the fact that the younger ones—all are men—are sent into town on buggering missions ("On les envoie prendre du dos en ville").

"Parade" means a circus parade before a performance, and the performance itself consists of a representation of the most bizarre mixture of creatures, times, and places: "sad ballads, tragedies about marauders and demigods"; "Chinese, Hottentots, gypsies, fools, hyenas, Molochs, old lunatics, sinister demons." Their secret science, "magnetic comedy," is a kind of magic, for the inventor of the theory of animal magnetism, Friedrich Anton Mesmer (whence "mesmerism"), conceived of the hypnotism he practiced as coming from an occult world force. The effect of magnetic comedy on the spectator is one of expansion of the scene and time: "Their eyes flame, their blood sings, their bones broaden, tears stream from their bloodshot eyes. Their jeers or their terror last a minute, or whole months."

The brilliant effect of hostility and secrecy conveyed by the poem comes initially from a contrast, implied in the phrase "your worlds," between *you*, the audience addressed, and *them*. The antithesis emerges more fully from the detached last line: "I alone have the key to this savage parade." Now the poet is identified with the secret powers of the "drôles très solides" and is separated from mankind by this inimical knowledge. The impression of a sinister elegance or beauty, matching their *science* and lurking violence, is especially well brought out in the description of the troupe: "What mature men! Eyes lethargic as a summer night, red and black, tricolored, of steel studded with golden stars; deformed features, leaden, livid, burnt out; joking hoarse voices! The cruel gait of spangles." The younger ones are dressed "with disgusting *luxury.*" The strange notations of color and metallic glints or shades express the mysteriousness of the whole poem: sinister, inexplicable mystery is one of the moods of certain *Illuminations* of the final phase and makes of them some of the most famous and brilliant poems of the cycle.

"Parade" may be read as a private fantasy about power, in which homosexuality symbolizes a separation from other men and hostility to them. This sexual reference is the opposite of the poems of heterosexual union and suggests that dichotomies underlie references to homosexuality: alienation from mankind corresponds to a form of inner discord. This theme is vividly rendered in "Vagabonds," in which the disharmony of the homosexual couple, recalling the pair of "Matinée d'ivresse," is matched by the speaker's dissatisfaction with himself.

In the "vigil" of "Vagabonds," which echoes the earlier poems of vigils in the *Illuminations*, the poet can magically create a "future nocturnal luxury" reminiscent of "Soir historique," but is frustrated in his major undertaking, the equivalent of the *œuvre* of "Matinée d'ivresse" and "Jeunesse," which is to return with his companion to the state of children of the sun, the sons of God in traditional symbolism (see, for example, Ephesians 5:8). This insistence on the past rather than the future of progress is reminiscent of Rimbaud's absorption in *vieillerie poétique* and pseudomysticism in the poems of 1872; the state of mind is the opposite of being "absolutely modern," in the phrase of *Une Saison.* The quest for man's primitive estate (alluded to in "Angoisse") is the philosophical equivalent of the search for an absolute and a statis, as opposed to the idea of the progressively expanding world of mental experiences, as in "Soir historique" or the first "Villes." Fate, however, holds the necessary *science* out of reach of the exiled poet, as in "Ouvriers"; this quest for individual salvation is doomed. The specific symbolism of failure is the poet's inability to find "the place and formula" for returning to mankind's original condition; magic represents in a sense a subjugation to the material, to the need of particular physical surroundings for it to work. The implicit contrast is strong with the places, especially the polar ones, which have been *found* by the poet, in the poems of illumination.

In "Vagabonds," we see with great clarity the symbolic sense of magic in the late *Illuminations*: the notion of an absolute, like that of the old metaphysics dismissed in "Dévotion," is translated into the mumbojumbo of spells. The only illumination possible is the inner harmony of "Métropolitain" or "Barbare," with implications of creativity, heterosexuality, and a perfect mental place. "Conte" transposes these notions into a fable about a *génie* and a prince. This *génie* shows Rimbaud's delicate manipulation of language, for he is a jinn rather than a *genius* like the *génie* of the eponymous earlier poem: the double etymology of *génie* is exploited. Jinns of course are the supernatural creatures of the Moslem world and are associated strongly with magic in the *Arabian Nights,* so that we have another symbol of the absolute or the metaphysics of transcendence. Since "Conte" is a fable, we are obliged by the genre to interpret it figuratively.

The prince of the fable feels he has exhausted heterosexuality in its traditional form and longs for "essential" desires and satisfaction, that is, for a metaphysical essence. This is a search for "truth," the key term of *Une Saison* being used here ironically for a kind of truth that does not exist. When the *génie* appears, he and the prince "were doubtless annihilated in an act of essential salubrity," their mutual orgasm. However, orgasm is not an essence or eternity, as "Matinée d'ivresse" reminds us, and so the prince, who was himself the *génie,* "passed away in his palace, at an ordinary age." The prince's form of narcissism makes an extraordinary parodic contrast to the heterosexual symbolism of wholeness and unity of the individual mind in "Métropolitain" or "Barbare." Another important reference is to elegance, *science*, and violence, the three qualities which play such a large role in the *Illuminations* of the first phase. The prince in his massacres tries to achieve a transcendent truth through violence; the *génie*'s beauty represents elegance, and the final line of the poem is a reference to *science* in the adjective *savante*: "La musique savante manque à notre désir"; that is, there is no science of harmony to fulfill us. We find here a notable contrast with a confident line in "Guerre": "C'est aussi simple qu'une phrase musicale," which refers to a conquest of the world accomplished with the aid of mathematics and logic.

The reason the *génie* is only the prince, in a vast self-delusion, lies in the inauthenticity of his desire for essences or absolute truths, which is identified with magic, with the idea of a *génie*-jinn, with homosexuality, and with the duality of body and spirit implied in the plot of this allegory. "Conte" describes an extreme form of the alienation from the condition of the individual and from the world which runs through the late *Illuminations*.

A fable like "Conte" can stand by itself, but certain *Illuminations* hardly seem to have any meaning apart from the body of the work; of none is this more true than of "Solde," which announces a clearance sale on all the renovated aspects of society seen in the first phase of *Illuminations*. These treasures are unknown to nobility and crime, cursed love and pedestrian honesty: they are beyond good and evil. They include the mathematics, reconstituted voices, harmony, and bodies of "Jeunesse"; the expansion of sensory perception, as in "Soir historique"; the migrations, sports, and *confort* of "Mouvement"; and, as in the first "Villes," a total satisfaction for the masses in which there are pleasures for every taste, such as a Romantic social system like Fourier's proposed. This figurative "sale on smuggled diamonds" refers to the images of that stone in "Angoisse" and perhaps in "Barbare." General words such as "énergies," "élan insensé et infini," "avenir," and "mouvement" recall the world of "Génie." The commercial and economic terms associated with the future in the first phase of the *Illuminations* are converted in "Solde" to a form of commerce which has the degrading associations of the shopworn, the unwanted stock, and the bargain basement. The life of the future and its luxuries, destined to delight the spirit as much as the body, are transformed into objects, an implied belittlement reinforced by the insistent repetition of "A vendre," "For Sale," and by the speaker's tone of hucksterism. Certainly there could be no point to this *Illumination* without the general theory of the structure of the whole which cyclic rise and fall provides.

The conclusion of "Solde" introduces a new element into the idea of a cyclic pattern: the wares are called "ce qu'on ne vendra jamais," and the speaker adds, ambivalently, that the stock is plentiful and that the traveling salesmen do not have to settle their accounts so soon. In other words, the speaker reverses the idea of the clearance sale: he is not disposing of all his merchandise, nor is he bankrupt. A movement back to the first phase of the *Illuminations* could begin, according to the principle of cyclic irony, by which nothing ever stays—or vanishes—forever. Recurrence is always possible. We shall encounter still further indications of reversal in these late *Illuminations*.

Rimbaud resorted once, in "Démocratie," to the use of quotation marks to show that the poem is ironic in title and content and that the method of the *Illuminations* consists, in part, of a shifting *I*, a multiple persona whom we can never point out as revealing a definitive form behind his many roles. This dramatic monologue complements "Ville" early in the cycle, for it depicts the other side of the unilluminated industrial society of the 19th century: colonialism.

"Le drapeau va au paysage immonde, et notre patois étouffe le tambour.

"Aux centres nous alimenterons la plus cynique prostitution. Nous massacrerons les révoltes logiques.

"Aux pays poivrés et détrempés! —au service des plus monstrueuses exploitations industrielles ou militaires.

"Au revoir ici, n'importe où. Conscrits du bon vouloir, nous aurons la philosophie féroce; ignorants pour la science, roués pour le confort; la crevaison pour le monde qui va. C'est la vraie marche. En avant, route!"

("The flag goes to the filthy landscape, and our patois drowns out the drum. In the towns we will encourage the most bestial prostitution. We will put down reasonable rebellions. To the wet and spicy countries! —in the service of the biggest kinds of industrial and military exploitation. Good-by here, anywhere. We are conscripts of good faith, our philosophy is merciless; ignorant of progress, wallowers in comfort; we say to hell with people in general. That's the real advance. Forward, march!")

The soldier of fortune has contempt for "logical" revolts, like the logical war in "Guerre"; he despises science, esteems comfort in its basest form, and does not want to hear of progress. The precise counterreference of the poem is found in the "en-marche" of "A une raison," with its army of new men marching into an illuminated future of love and harmony. The allegorical "A une raison" and the realistic monologue of "Démocratie" form a striking antithesis in their styles.

With "Enfance" we reach the longest *Illumination*, but the parallelisms among its five parts are such that the poem is not so difficult to apprehend as a whole as certain shorter ones. We recall that the speaker of "Ouvriers" had had a partly miserable childhood, and the poet of "Enfance" evokes series of images of alienation, many of them evidently a child's fantasy. We recall also that the speaker of "Aube" is a child and that there is a single child in "Après le déluge"; childhood, as in "Les Poètes de sept ans," has a distinct implication of heightened perception in certain poems of Rimbaud, though no particular *dérèglement des sens* is present.

In Part I a sensual and exotic female figure appears, and she is called an "idol," which is a pejorative variant upon the idea of a goddess. Then women of all kinds—young mothers, princesses, big sisters—are evoked, only for the poem to break off in disgust at heterosexuality conceived of in its old sentimental form: "What a bore, the time for talk about 'your dear body' and 'your dear heart.'" Progressive rejection or being rejected is the pattern of "Enfance," and Part II deals with spatial symbols of alienation. There is a landscape from which man is absent, but which is filled momentarily by the delusion of magic: "Des fleurs magiques bourdonnaient." Part III, with its list of nouns preceded by *il y a*, indicates fascinating presences, which abruptly vanish at the words "Finally, when you are hungry and thirsty, there is someone to drive you away." The sense of an imaginary quest for satisfaction grows increasingly stronger in "Enfance"; Part IV contains a series of fantasies which begin with fulfillment of a kind ("I am the saint"; "I am the scholar"), then evoke a horizontal movement into the distance, as the speaker becomes a traveler on foot or a child drifting out to sea. Finally, the walker reaches the end of the world:

> Les sentiers sont âpres. Les monticules se couvrent de genêts. L'air est immobile. Que les oiseaux et les sources sont loin! Ce ne peut être que la fin du monde, en avançant.
>
> (The paths are rough. Broom is covering the hills. The air is motionless. How far away the birds and springs are! It can only be the end of the world ahead.)

The sense of nothingness is remarkably rendered. Rimbaud's fondness for unusual geographical or cosmological images is marked in "Enfance"; the fantasy of reaching the end of the world is followed by one of subterranean isolation in Part V, in which the speaker, in boredom and bitterness, inhabits an underground drawing room. Reversal is implied in the last line of the poem: "Why should a ghostly vent appear, pale, in the corner of the vault?" If it should appear—the conditional tense is remotely hypothetical —the speaker would rejoin mankind, as is symbolized by the vent linking his cell with the earth's surface. Such an event would start a new cycle, which would doubtless end again, eventually, in alienation.

"Vies" contrasts with the positive "Jeunesse" and the negative "Enfance" in that it deals with an old man, who gives three parallel accounts of his life. He has acquired *science* in the Holy Land and in an obscure passageway in Paris, reinvented love in a new musical form, and seen all times and places in the attic in which he was shut up as a child; this last imagery is a variant of the solitary visions of "Jeunesse." Each section of "Vies" ends with an indication first of exile or retirement, then of a change in the life of the world or the old man: "What is my insignificance compared with your coming stupor?" "I am given over to a new nervous ailment—I expect to become a very nasty madman." "I have been charged with another task. I mustn't think any more of all that. I am really from beyond the tomb, and no messages transmitted." The obscurity of these lines does not prevent our seizing that movement—and possibly cyclic movement—is their real point. The old man's end is a new beginning.

IV

One of the greatest hindrances to reading Rimbaud lies in a lack of broad historical perspective on 19th-century literature and thought and in the acceptance of unexamined received images like that of the drunken Rimbaud or the Rimbaud raving in drug-induced states. One critic, for example, concludes his survey of Wordsworthian elements in Romantic literature with a contrasting and parodic picture of Rimbaud despising nature and forcing himself into sodomy to reach a Manichean deity. These picturesque clichés fall apart, as well as does that of Romantic poetry tending towards the Wordsworthian, when we look seriously into German and French Romantic poetry and into Blake. Instead of the imagination substituting for God and heightening the experience of nature, Hölderlin believed in a radical transcendence in which nature as such plays little role; Novalis' ideas included both the theory of nature as correspondences, as a book rather than as something in itself, and a very strange conception of transcendence. Hugo's theology was double, for he juxtaposed a Neoplatonic occultist metaphysics of light to a mystery in which evil seems to dominate. Baudelaire changed the thought patterns of *Les Fleurs du mal* from a book of normal correspondence in the first edition to a Manichean form of Christianity in the second one, which is the edition of *Les Fleurs du mal* we read today. Finally, Blake did away with the transcendent in a theology which, though aphoristic and explicit in many ways, is so complex a system that quite opposite interpretations of it still persist.

When we have made the effort to study the major poetic theologies of the 19th century, our sense of what Rimbaud's thinking consists of is greatly sharpened. We see the general absence of a formal system of correspondences, for example, and above all the disinclination to exalt mystery, especially in the *Illuminations.* Rimbaud's otherworldly picture of nature in 1872 reminds one of Novalis' contention that our ultimate view of the world should be of the *vieillerie poétique* of a *Märchen* or fairy tale, with its naïveté and supernatural. The dualistic interpretation of Christianity found in *Une Saison* is readily seen in Baudelaire's work, while Blake's poetry and prose offer suggestive parallels with Rimbaud's, if we eliminate the concept of the imagination, which, in a developed form, was, by and large, foreign to French thought.

The identification of God and man in Blake, the rejection of transcendence, and the breaking down of the dualism of good and evil are accompanied by other thoughts in which we see the relationship between Blake's poetic system and the formal theological writings of Schleiermacher. Romantic conceptions of religion stress freedom, as opposed to the master-and-slave hierarchy of orthodox thought. As important as the orthodox metaphysical ideas of man and God is the slave morality, the psychology of Christianity, to which is opposed a sense of the universe, of totality. With this sense of unity as an experience or feeling goes the notion that God is present in human self-consciousness, thought, and action.[11] Placing God and the world in the content of one's mind rather than in an external spatial metaphysics allows for the conception of a non-transcendent Idea working itself out in man's social history. The feeling of immanence is substituted for pantheism with its spatial implications, and time may be perceived subjectively and varyingly, so that eternity takes the form of an experience, not a metaphysical concept.

If we follow Blakean lines and read the *Illuminations* in psychological rather than metaphysical, transcendent terms, we find that the first phase, with its emphasis on building, has a mental character like the rest: "Mental Things alone are Real." "Man has no Body distinct from his Soul; for that Call'd Body is a portion of Soul discern'd by the five senses."[12] I am certain that after the experience of the pseudo-transcendent in 1872, Rimbaud retained the notion, already present in the second *lettre du voyant*, that mind and idea color the bodily and the external, when they do not generate their own content. Certainly the important position of "Génie" among the poems alluding to building, to Saint-Simonianism, and to the future confirms this, for in "Génie" the content is ethical and psychological, with no reference to the practical, material side of life, which is secondary and subordinate to a state of mind.

The idea of mental vision and increased perception which preoccupied Blake shows up in the descriptive *Illuminations* of the second phase. These are not all concerned with beauty in the ordinary sense, but rather with the idea of the strange adventures which use of the mental eye procures. Allegorically, they can be said to represent a satisfaction for the individual beyond his conception of illumination for mankind expressed in "Génie" and "Mouvement." A solitary, untroubled self, higher than that of the wretched, isolated speakers of "Ville" or "Ouvriers," experiences the visions of the second phase.

Some increased tension between the activities of men and the poet ("Being Beauteous," the opening of "Métropolitain") ushers in quieter allegories of unity of mind, which goes along with a sense of concentration of forces: the polar imagery, as at the end of "Métropolitain," represents the old symbolism of the center, the place where spiritual powers are most intense. Literal heterosexuality and union with the feminine symbol of the mind also represent this unity, which is, furthermore, a unity of man and the divine immanence, suggested by the earthly location of the female presence. At the same time, in "Fairy," Rimbaud uses touches of the old transcendent imagery of the Queen of Heaven (see Jeremiah 44:17, 25), the female deity associated with the cosmos by way of stars.

In the concluding phase of the *Illuminations*, nature is revealed as a fatal cycle governing man, who is subjected to uncontrollable alternations of moods and the biological determinism of aging. Division and alienation are as natural as unity, proceeding as they do from the cosmic principle of divisions following union. In the *Illuminations*, nature does not appear so much in the form of landscapes as in that of universal process, a hardly exceptional representation of nature in the Romantics, if we think of the degree to which correspondences or transcendent imagery dominate the work of Hölderlin, Novalis, Baudelaire, and Hugo—or of Blake's theological indifference to the natural.

These observations on the sense of the *Illuminations*, which are drawn from points of similarity and contrast with Blake and other Romantics, in regard to the nature of Rimbaud's symbolism and theology, are incomplete without a more precise description of Rimbaud's peculiar cyclic form, which does not culminate in an apocalypse after the fashion of Blake and others. Nor is it quite the anti-apocalypse, the sense of hopeless loss of revelation found in Hölderlin's poetry, that characterizes the last phase of the *Illuminations*. It is, in fact, in regard to the question of cyclic form that Rimbaud departs from Romantic practice and establishes his exemplarity for more modern literature.

There are complex relationships between the individual poems of the *Illuminations*. We have seen the shifting connotations of words such as *violence*, which can be related to *force*, a term which, in turn, can evoke an idea like *œuvre*, in the course of its repetitions. The spatial conceptions of the poems vary considerably both in regard to world or cosmic space and in more localized treatments of it, as in the linear involution of "Ponts" and the simple setting of "Royauté." The speaker has a range of masks or characters, and the persons and pronouns he uses do not vary any less: besides the shifts we have noted, there are such anomalies as the change within "Aube" from first to third person near the end, for an effect of distancing and altered perceptual mode. Certain gaps exist in the *Illuminations* as well; the idea of man's primitive state of freedom is only irregularly referred to, as is the idea of a test or trial, which we see most succinctly in "Royauté." In poetic method, we find not only a variety of styles juxtaposed, but also a varying use of symbolism and allegory. The players of "Parade" illustrate the moods, attitudes, and desires of the speaker of the poem, while "Démocratie" has a literal sense and can be called symbolic only in that its representation of colonialism is part of a pattern by which the illuminated world and the unilluminated actual world are contrasted. "Démocratie," furthermore, illustrates the fact that certain poems are virtually meaningless without the whole of the *Illuminations*, by which various words and ideas acquire the vividness produced by crossreferences. Even when a poem can stand by itself, like "Mouvement," with its traditional symbolism, the fact that its title connects it with the themes of "Génie" greatly enriches it. Elsewhere, we are more aware of disparities, like that between the cycles suggested by "Matinée d'ivresse" or "A une raison" and the total cyclic form.

The coexistence of seemingly antithetical themes is one ironic dimension of the *Illuminations* which the cyclic pattern resolves, even though there persists the effect we have called cyclic irony: the sense of impermanence and recurrence. Thus we find the contrast between the polar imagery of coldness, lucidity, and concentration, on the one hand, and, on the other, the theme of magic and the unattainable in the concluding *Illuminations*. However, when we examine each group of poems more carefully, we discover various modifying elements in them that make the overall contrasts far from simple. To take the poems of union or polar imagery, we observe that, beginning with the implicit pastness of the first "Villes," there occur indications of past time, especially verbs in the *passé simple* as in "Métropolitain," "Royauté," and "Aube," which suggest some tension between a present speaker and the remoteness of the events or state described. The contrast between presentness and memory is a subtle kind of division between body and mind, a dwelling on a unity which once was, but implicitly exists no longer. Even in "Barbare," which lacks a main verb, the parenthetical "elles n'existent pas," said of the flowers, provides such a tension amid images of calm and mental wholeness.

If we turn now to an opposing group of poems, those of magic, we sense another form of the same tension. In ideas of magic, the mind soars above reality; there is a search for an absolute, in an attempt to reverse isolation and ennui. But the desire to escape solitude has a certain analogy with poems of positive construction like "Jeunesse" or "Angoisse." The difference lies in that magic would provide a true absolute, far beyond the cyclic satisfaction of "Génie" or the moment of lucidity at the pole, as in "Métropolitain," or in the palm garden of "Royauté." However, the difference is not a strict antithesis, but a thematic modification. The ironies which run through the *Illuminations* are a unifying element, even though they are not exactly of the same kind. Formal irony—the conclusion of a poem which marks a shift in direction, a cancellation, or a reversal of the preceding theme—is found everywhere in the *Illuminations*. Much the same notion of modification applies to the idea of nature as a fateful wheel or of the cosmic as consisting in an eternal series of recurrences, with which one should identify oneself in austere joy: there is a difference of perspective and mood, more than a total antithesis, as there would be between a cycle and stasis. Irony can be a reaction to satisfactions which do not endure or a reaction to despair that one wishes to conjure away, but irony itself has different degrees and forms which do not correspond to joy or despair, and so we find ourselves in the presence of irregular relationships in the *Illuminations* rather than of easy antitheses.

With the prevalence of ironic forms and the presence of cyclic poems within a large cycle, we realize that the total form of the *Illuminations*, while perceptible, is unstable, with its indefinite cyclical perspective. Rimbaud made sure, by his verbs, that the poems of union would not form a fixed point to which everything else would simply refer. The result is, in the currently fashionable term, a "decentered" work, like *Finnegans Wake*, with which the *Illuminations* have curious resemblances in the use of cyclic notions and abundant ironies, or like the *Cantos*, which are coextensive with Pound's life and therefore have no truly autonomous structure. The *Illuminations* are not clearer or simpler by the principle that clarity misrepresents the things it undertakes to clarify—a dangerous principle, but one sufficiently justified by the artistic success of the work.

V

I have observed that cyclic forms can be found in Rimbaud's work as early as "Soleil et chair," the whole of which constitutes a cycle of historical and spiritual renewal after a fall. There are hints of this pattern in the allusions in the *Illuminations* to an early "franchise première" and a future of renewal. The first cyclic poems, however, in which Rimbaud's gifts are completely in evidence are "Le Bateau ivre" and "Mémoire," if the latter is at all earlier than the other poems of 1872 we possess. "Le Bateau ivre" contains the first example of the natural cycle, that is, the necessary ending of a course of action or life in dispersal of energy or aging and death; it is easy to perceive how this cycle, made more elaborate by subtler distinctions and shades of feeling, forms the basis for the declining phase of the cycle of the *Illuminations*. "Mémoire," which deals with a historical and individual fall, receives its cyclic effect from recurrence of imagery in variant forms; it consists, in fact, of only the first two of the three stages of the kind of cycle found in "Soleil et chair": primitive freedom, fall, and achievement of a higher form of the primordial state.

The poems of 1872 must have come to form a cycle in an initially unintentional fashion: to the extent that they are autobiographical, the end of Rimbaud's experiment and experience could not have been anticipated at the beginning. This highly original adaptation of the metaphysics of light and other mystical motifs consists of a pattern of rise and imminent fall, the latter recorded in "O saisons, ô châteaux." Both from "O saisons" and from the commentary in *Une Saison en enfer*, we gather that the declining phase of the cycle constitutes another form of the natural pattern of growth, fullness and decay: physical deterioration and the threat of death conclude it.

Rimbaud was a poet dominated by ideas from the beginning, but it is only with the poems of 1872 that he synthesized a quite unfamiliar-seeming kind of cycle, in which the conception of poetry as a form of epistemology is carried well beyond the adventures of the *bateau ivre*, with their more simple and obvious analogies with the course of life. The hints of the *lettres du voyant* about new forms and perceptual derangement are realized, as well as the cyclic idea of the "horribles travailleurs," who will sink under the weight of their visions, as Rimbaud tells it in the second *lettre du voyant*, only to be relayed by other thiefs of fire.

It is characteristic of Rimbaud that the critique of the poems of 1872— and of the Manichean Christianity Rimbaud detected behind them—should also take the form of a cycle, but this time one of descent into hell and emergence on the far side of it. *Une Saison* marks the intellectual liquidation of Rimbaud's experience during his affair with Verlaine. The breadth of this shared quest can best be judged by the fact that it led Verlaine, who, however involved, played poetically a secondary role to Rimbaud, from skepticism to the beginning of a conversion of the most orthodox sort. We can scarcely evaluate the full extent of Rimbaud's new orientation in 1872 because of the loss of at least one key poem, but the reaction to it, ultimately revealed in *Une Saison*, is so massive in its violence and irony as to make us wary of underestimating it.

There are images and themes in the last sections of *Une Saison* which we find again in the *Illuminations*; the "new work" is one of them, and they demonstrate the overlap between *Une Saison* and *Illuminations*. However, the *Illuminations* bear witness, more so than *Une Saison*, to the richness and variety of Rimbaud's intellectual life from 1870 on; we can find traces of ideas of every phase of his career in them, but their art is so advanced as to make one incline to date them from 1873 and 1874 rather than from any earlier time. Moreover, the four-phasal order I find in them suggests a lengthy and complex maturation, in which Rimbaud saw how he could combine the most antithetical thematic material in one work—for the manuscript was given to Verlaine in Stuttgart in 1875 as a work, I am sure, not as a miscellany. Finally, the cyclical patterns which had contained and informed previous specific concepts like the *dérèglement des sens* or magic mysticism are made infinitely convoluted in the *Illuminations*. Rimbaud's cyclical patterns, the superstructure of his work, are doubled and superimposed: the pattern of descent and rise, on which *Une Saison* is built, is coupled with that of ascension and fall, but in such a way that they are eternally repetitive and reciprocal. This, I think, is as thoroughgoing an example as one could find of patterns of thought whose shape stands out above any specific content.

With Mallarmé, however, we shall encounter yet another example of a poet in whom a general shaping of thought will provide a guiding thread through a very diverse, very brilliantly varied poetic production, but with Mallarmé there will be a store of essays, of carefully phrased thoughts to support and connect the poems.

Chapter IV

MALLARMÉ IN THE 1860s

I

Mallarmé's early life has been scrutinized for material of psychoanalytic interest, such as the deaths of his mother and sister, but for a poet who was so conscious of esthetic values, attempts to uncover a hidden chain of meanings in his work necessarily remain tangential to his undertaking. Mallarmé's intellectual development was complex, but followed a certain logic or dialectic of creativity, and my purpose is to apprehend the stages of it with as much accuracy as possible. Much as in the case of Rimbaud, the significant patterns in his work depend on his powerful and critical intellect rather than on some expression of the unconscious.

At the point where Mallarmé emerged from the varied early influences on his poetry,[1] we find that his verse, substantially that published in the first *Parnasse contemporain*, shows dualisms reflecting Baudelaire's "spleen et idéal": depression and creativity, the real and the ideal. These oppositions are mentioned in the correspondence (I, 90),[2] where we find, furthermore, a suggestion that the vagueness of life contrasts with the formal beauty of poetry (I, 149; December 1864). In other words, the widespread Romantic moral and psychological antitheses which Baudelaire richly exploited have evolved towards a more purely esthetic conception, in which the ideal is both the poet's creative state of mind and the structured work he produces. Many dualisms, however, represent merely one moment of a dialectic or tripartite pattern. Cyclic and threefold movements are to be discerned, whether explicit or implicit, at various points in Mallarmé's thought.

The prose piece "Symphonie littéraire" (written 1864), ostensibly about Gautier, Baudelaire, and Banville, can be read, in terms of its imagery, as a prose poem concerning a version of the para-Christian myth of paradise (represented by ancient Greece and Banville), the fall (into an inorganic world, found in Baudelaire's poetry), and a resurrection (through reading Gautier) into a serene, spiritual heaven, which is yet of this world. The "symphony" of the title might be considered to be the overtones which constitute the myth and which emanate from the specific appreciations of the three poets' verse. From this central myth derive poems which form variations on it. "Les Fenêtres" alludes to paradise, the "ciel antérieur," and its angel poet is afraid of falling like Satan instead of achieving a new life. The religious symbolism is pursued in "Le Sonneur"; paradise and an etiolated fallen life recur in "Les Fleurs." The fall, ironically, constitutes the matter of the poet's work in "Le Pitre châtié," where he is incapable of rising to the pure heights of rebirth. The paradisaical childhood which the poet of "Las de l'amer repos" fled in order to cultivate a tortured, fallen night poetry will be matched by his eventual attainment of an impersonal "Chinese" form of pastoral art. This contrast between two kinds of poetry, one of tormented or Baudelairean imagery and one achieving the serene tone of Banville, is carried beyond "Symphonie littéraire" and "Las de l'amer repos": such a distinction will characterize *Hérodiade*, Mallarmé's winter poem, in contrast to "L'Après-midi d'un faune," which he worked on in the summer (I, 166), while resting from the struggle with *Hérodiade*.

The tendency towards thinking in sharp antitheses, so common in French Romantic literature, is characteristic of certain early poems of Mallarmé in which the tripartite scheme is reduced to a present contrast between life and creation: "L'Azur" is the finest example of this. The opposition of a depressing life and exhilarating creativity is associated with the antithesis between men as a whole and the artist, which Mallarmé explored in the early "Hérésies artistiques: L'Art pour tous" (published in 1862). Poetry should have "hieratic" or hermetic ways of expression, and Mallarmé envies the cryptic notation of music (whose ambiguities like enharmonic writing would have delighted him, had he been aware of them).

In "Hérésies artistiques" Mallarmé alludes to the once understood technical nature of poetry, and we find a covert allusion to rhetoric, a word so exclusively pejorative in 19th-century use as to make it unavailable to positive conceptions of poetry. Be that as it may, it was rhetoric that formerly constituted the métier of poetry, comparable to the technical disciplines of sculpture or music, and, as confirmation of Mallarmé's secret allusion to rhetoric, we need only analyze the style of "L'Azur," with its very prominent figures, or the even more elaborate texture of the later "Ouverture ancienne" of *Hérodiade*, which Mallarmé felt to be his masterpiece up to then (April 1866 [I, 207]). The latter employs hendiadys, hyperbaton, synecdoche, hypallage, and the rare epanalepsis ("De qui le long regret et les tiges de qui"), among other rhetorical devices.

There are important references to composition or poetic structures in the letters of the 1860s (I, 211, 117), including a rhetorical explication of "L'Azur" (I, 103-05). Poe's "Philosophy of Composition" supplies the authority for viewing poems as structures. However, composition in the normal 19th-century sense is dispositio, the traditional rhetorical conception of the thematic relation of parts to the whole. It is a valid esthetic principle, but one not likely to lead to the more complex notions of linguistic unity presupposed by modern poetry. Poe's expressive and anti-mimetic tendencies were carried much further by Mallarmé when he began working on *Hérodiade*: here he wanted to paint not things, but the effect they produce on one (I, 137). This is a technical idea of great power, since it implies a dominance of figurative psychological language in which the perceived may merge with non-perceptual material in the perceiver's mind. In a stage piece or monologue like *Hérodiade* or "L'Après-midi d'un faune," the depiction of subjective effect suggests the portraying of consciousness in depth. It is interesting to see that as a complement to his highly thematic notion of the poem's design Mallarmé evolved a psychological one; yet this psychological conception is strictly esthetic and not dependent on extra-literary ideas.

It is important to observe that despite his "literary symphony" Mallarmé is basically not tempted, as yet at least, to describe poetry in terms of something else, whether it be music, painting, architecture or a philosophical conception. To be sure, the religious connotations of "artistic heresy," the angelism of "Les Fenêtres," and other theological allusions color the whole poetic enterprise, but Mallarmé has a lucid notion of poetry as an art, with its proper technical resources. Such clear-sightedness is most rare in the history of 19th-century French esthetic ideas: on the one hand, Hugo early compared poetry with the plastic arts, and poets like Gautier pursued the analogy; on the other hand, Baudelaire was never able to focus on technical matters in discussing poetry, for they always dissolved into ethical and psychological considerations. With no precedents and no critical language to draw upon, Mallarmé managed to orient himself precisely in respect to the problems confronting him.

The larger question of the unity and independence of poetry leads to various ramifications of thought in Mallarmé's letters of the mid-1860s. The unity of poetry is unrelated to the accidental, contingent character of life and of any real mimesis of it. We find here another of the analogies with theology so typical of Mallarmé's thought: in traditional philosophical terms, God's existence may be posited as a necessary cause and contrast to the world's contingency. Similarly, in poetry we find the absolute which is lacking in life. This opposition between poetry and life is obviously not completely tenable on a practical plane, so Mallarmé distinguishes between pure poetry like his and the ordinary lyrical conception of verse, as in the work of his friend Emmanuel des Essarts, where "chance" and cliché determine the wording. Chance is the contrary of structure.

Since structure is a matter of craft, the poet can change styles (I, 154), which have no necessary inspirational basis. The poet sees words as distinctive materials out of which he builds the poem: *Hérodiade* is a dark red word (I, 154) and must be joined with suitable terms. The lyrical conception of poetry, on the other hand, is to see words as conventional counters for conventional feelings, such as love (I, 155-56). Lyricism in the ordinary 19th-century sense mistakes journalistic, mimetic language for poetry. In the latter, as Mallarmé finally discovered when working on *Hérodiade*, words reflect one another by their various esthetic properties (I, 234); therein lies the unity of the poem, which is independent, ultimately, of the simpler kind of thematic coherence. At the same time, we must note that the esthetic properties of words, as we may see from Mallarmé's poems, consist in a complicated relationship of signifier and signified: mellifluous nonsense could not be further from Mallarmé's goal. A new complexity of subject matter, in fact, matches Mallarmé's increasing sophistication of stylistic theory.

In regard to the themes or paraphrasable content of the poem, antithetical thinking sharpens one's sense of the various aspects of life and poetry, but it is ultimately rather frustrating in that one is constantly tossed between opposing elements with little hope of that philosophical repose so prized by the makers of systems, philosophical and poetical. As Mallarmé conceived more and more strongly of the formal linguistic effect of the poem, he came also to reject the dualisms of his early work such as "L'Azur." Antithesis might be said to be a preliminary or premature form of thought. Mallarmé's resolution of oppositions—for he was to move towards unity and harmony of intellectual design—did not come about by one decisive philosophical act, but rather through an evolution which began with "L'Après-midi d'un faune" and moved through *Hérodiade* and beyond, in a prolonged crisis of thought.

A new sense of linguistic unity and pattern is apparent in "L'Après-midi d'un faune." Through its three versions, the poem kept as its thematic material the contrast between illusion and reality, the faun sleeping and awake, and the nymphs as a mirage created by pink roses or in their fleshly reality. The poem is basically antithetical, but by using more than one antithesis, Mallarmé is able to give the impression of a much more complex structure and to sustain its substantial length. Essentially, however, "L'Après-midi" moves by oppositions and ends with a circular effect, by which the faun

falls asleep as he had awakened in the beginning—the cyclical design suggesting something more intricate than antithesis. At the same time, the antitheses are of a psychological rather than metaphysical order: the faun is
exploring his own mind rather than cosmic principles, and there is therefore none of the philosophical impasse of early poems such as "L'Azur."
Mallarmé's psychological imagery, the recording of impressions rather than
things, shows up in the elaborately ambiguous language, as when memories
of cool water and a breeze left by the nymphs' presence are cogitated by
the faun into the metaphorical results of his panpipes:

> Faune, l'illusion s'échappe des yeux bleus
> Et froids, comme une source en pleurs, de la plus chaste:
> Mais, l'autre tout soupirs, dis-tu qu'elle contraste
> Comme brise du jour chaude dans ta toison?

(Faun, the illusion escapes from the blue and cold eyes of the chaster one. But do
you think that the other, with her sighs, contrasts with the first like a warm daytime
breeze in your fleece?)

The faun seems to ask if the nymphs suggested the landscape, but sense
would demand here that he wonder whether, on the contrary, the landscape did not create the illusion of nymphs. Natural sense and idiom counter each other in an ambiguity that reveals the faun's subrational train of
thought, where unexpected reversals are to be countenanced. He continues:

> Que non! par l'immobile et lasse pâmoison
> Suffoquant de chaleurs le matin frais s'il lutte,
> Ne murmure point d'eau que ne verse ma flûte
> Au bosquet arrosé d'accords; et le seul vent
> Hors des deux tuyaux prompt à s'exhaler avant
> Qu'il disperse le son dans une pluie aride,
> C'est, à l'horizon pas remué d'une ride,
> Le visible et serein souffle artificiel
> De l'inspiration, qui regagne le ciel.

(No! In the motionless faint weariness of noon, suffocating the struggling morning
with heat, there is no water murmuring other than that poured out by my flute over
the thicket bathed in harmonies. And the only wind, aside from that rapidly exhaled
from my pipes—before it disperses sounds in a dry rain—is, on the unmoving horizon,
the visible, tranquil, and art-creating breath of inspiration as it rises to heaven.)

The faun at once affirms the reality of the figurative water and breeze of
his music and seems to deny that such a reality could have suggested the
presence of nymphs. Yet we immediately realize that his singing of nymphs,
which he is to repeat shortly, would be yet another explanation for the
illusion—if it was one. As in the earlier lines, we find a complex, often paradoxical interplay of logical, verbal, and psychological factors. The traditional concepts of composition and rhetorical figuration, which Mallarmé

employed in analyzing "L'Azur," are no longer adequate for the description of so elusive a linguistic structure. However, one may readily analyze the subject of "L'Après-midi d'un faune," despite stylistic complexities. In *Hérodiade*, on the other hand, Mallarmé was much more sure of his new verbal accomplishment than of its subject, in the ordinary sense.

Whereas Mallarmé early defined "L'Après-midi" as having a symbolic subject, the problematic *Hérodiade* seems to have first presented itself to his mind in terms of a certain complex texture and color rather than as being organized around one single principle. "Impressions follow one another as in a symphony" (I, 161). "Impression" (which of course had nothing as yet to do with the history of painting) is often Mallarmé's term for figurative language; and as for the comparison with music, symphonic concerts were not yet a staple of musical life in France, and Mallarmé seems not to mean by symphony a pattern like sonata form so much as a multiplicity of voices woven together. The method of *Hérodiade* cannot really be compared to the more obviously antithetical one of "L'Après-midi," and the problems of sequence in imagery seem to have taken such precedence in Mallarmé's mind that he did not really see where the poem was leading him. Perhaps he at first conceived of *Hérodiade* as a rather decorative piece of verse, but later he realized that in the poem he had devised something impersonal and about beauty (I, 193, 215) and at the same time had filled it secretly with his entire being (I, 221). "Don du poème" conveys not the sense of *Hérodiade*, but rather the tortured character of the compositional process:

> Je t'apporte l'enfant d'une nuit d'Idumée!
> Noire, à l'aile saignante et pâle, déplumée.

(I bring you the child of an Idumean night! Black, with a bloody, pale, featherless wing.)

This defeathered monster recalls the "featherless wings" of the poet of "Les Fenêtres," who unwittingly commits a Satanic act and falls through all eternity. *Hérodiade* plunged Mallarmé unexpectedly into all manner of theoretical questions.

In April 1866, after three months of intense work on *Hérodiade*, Mallarmé took a short vacation in Cannes with his friend Eugène Lefébure, whom we find referred to both as a Hegelian (I, 218n) and as one interested in Indian philosophy (I, 210). The doubts about the nature and possibility of poetry that were beginning to assail Mallarmé were stimulated in the direction of philosophical inquiry by Lefébure's conversation, and for two years Mallarmé was to theorize about art in relation to more general ontological questions. At first, Mallarmé's orientation is like that of Buddhism, in the sense that he sees Nothingness beneath the veil of Becoming, yet resorts to an ethical idealism:

> Yes, I know, we are only empty forms of matter, but very sublime ones for having invented God and our own souls. So sublime, my friend, that I want to contemplate the spectacle of matter, conscious of being and yet leaping frantically into the ideal which it knows doesn't exist, singing . . . in the face of the Nothingness which is truth, these glorious lies!
>
> Such is the plan of my lyrical volume and such will perhaps be its title: *La Gloire du mensonge*, or *Le Glorieux Mensonge*. (I, 207-08)

Given the fact that Henri Cazalis, to whom these lines were addressed, later wrote about Indian philosophy in *Le Livre du néant* (1872), which was to include a section entitled "La Gloire du néant," it is surprising that Mallarmé, familiar as he must have been with Cazalis' ideas, should have claimed not to have known Buddhism at the moment when Nothingness most fully presented itself to his thought (I, 207). He was to encourage Cazalis in the latter's plans for a book on Nothingness (I, 243, 320) and himself conceived at one moment of a work called *Somptuosités du néant.* In any case, the thought of Nothingness put a momentary end to Mallarmé's work on *Hérodiade*, despite his attempt to rise above it by proclaiming the glory of illusion.

What we gather from the correspondence, placing together the picture from later letters as well as from the important one quoted above, is that human activities, including the making of poetry, began to seem more and more idle and vain, as Mallarmé struggled with the technical difficulties of *Hérodiade*. There are various ways to solve the problem of an all-invading sense of Nothingness. One is the renunciation of activity, as Schopenhauer preached, although the latter admitted himself that his philosophy was more theoretical than practical. The achievement of the sublime peace of nirvana is the Buddhist solution, but does not always suit the occidental temperament. Cazalis was to recommend that we glory in illusion: "We are on earth to give ourselves for a moment the illusion of eternity, to make our desires and dreams seem infinite, despite the narrow bonds of life . . . so that Nature will be aware of her grandeur in our consciousnesses—aware also of her wretchedness, of ever-fleeting reality and ever-present Nothingness" (*Le Livre du néant*, "La Gloire du néant," p. 64). The paradox of Cazalis' thought is a trifle unsatisfying, however, and Mallarmé's "Buddhist" attitude was to be of short duration, although he continued to insist on the importance of having perceived the nullity of existence.

A month after his stay in Cannes, Mallarmé was reproved by Cazalis for his treatment of Being and Nothingness as reciprocal concepts (I, 217n). Lefébure was shortly to ask if Mallarmé was still juggling the ideas of Being,

Nothingness, and the Absolute,[3] so that we perceive that, from the original antithesis between man's nullity and his ideals, Mallarmé has proceeded to a kind of dialectic solution of the ontological problem as he formulated it. However, it is Beauty, rather than the more general term of Absolute, which first presented itself to Mallarmé's mind as the synthesis of Being and Nothingness: "After finding Nothingness, I found Beauty" (I, 220). Beauty is the true meaning of *Hérodiade*, which Mallarmé had not realized until Nothingness had become such an obsession that he was obliged to think through the problem with the philosophical tools at his disposal.

Hérodiade has a curious relation to Mallarmé's theorizing, given the way its meaning seemed to grow out of the parallel processes of writing verse and thinking discursively. The poem has a general allegorical sense, made clear finally by the publication in our day of Mallarmé's late sketches for the completion of it;[4] at the same time, we may perceive a covert or inner significance in *Hérodiade* which is no less rich.

On the surface, it is not difficult to explain the dialectic of *Hérodiade* in terms of the poem's vocabulary. One can easily draw up lists of symbolic associations. For Hérodiade herself, these are variously abstraction, other-worldliness, the state of being an object, an existence as potentiality, Nothingness, night, cold, winter, the subterranean, and the inorganic. For Saint John, as he appears in anticipation in the "Scène" from *Hérodiade* and in the posthumous "Cantique de Saint Jean," the contrasting characteristics are concreteness, this-worldliness, the function of a perceiving subject, activity (as agent he sees Hérodiade), Being, noon, heat, the summer solstice (Saint John's Day), flesh, and blood. (The verbal design, which I have rendered here so schematically, perfectly illustrates Mallarmé's ultimate theory of poetic language as consisting of words reflecting one another in complicated patterns.) The union at sunset in a kind of marriage of Hérodiade and Saint John's head stands for realized beauty. The artist, become impersonal, as is symbolized by Saint John's decapitation, joins with beauty in its otherness or non-human phase, to transcend the limits of human beingness.

Such a scheme is perfectly coherent, but it fails to account for the peculiar tone of the poem, especially of the two sections written in the 1860s ("Ouverture ancienne" and "Scène"). We find there an overwhelming insistence on ancient dying things. Although Hérodiade is herself young, she is surrounded by a decaying manor which the old nurse describes in "Ouverture ancienne," a piece which appeared to Mallarmé as his greatest poetic achievement when he was working on it:

Abolie, et son aile affreuse dans les larmes
Du bassin, aboli, qui mire les alarmes
Des ors nus fustigeant l'espace cramoisi,
Une Aurore a, plumage, héraldique, choisi
Notre tour cinéraire et sacrificatrice

. . . .

Ah! des pays déchus et tristes le manoir!
Pas de clapotement! L'eau morne se résigne,
Que ne visite plus la plume ni le cygne
Inoubliable: l'eau reflète l'abandon
De l'automne éteignant en elle son brandon.

(An uncertain dawn, like a heraldic bird, has chosen to rest on our funereal and sacrificial tower, with its dreadful wing in the tears of the uncertain pool, where the cries of bare gold whipping the crimson sky are reflected . . . . Ah, the manor of sad and fallen lands! No ripple on the water! The dreary water, no longer visited by the swan's feathery wing, grows still in resignation; it reflects the departure of autumn which has extinguished its torch in it.)

Aboli might be said to have the sense of "passing into Nothingness" in Mallarmé's poetic idiom. Furthermore, ancient things (described variously as *vieillot, désuet,* and *fané*) haunted Mallarmé as early as the prose poems "Frisson d'hiver," "Plainte d'automne," and "Le Démon de l'analogie." In his personal life, Mallarmé had become obsessed with watching himself age in the mirror (I, 142, 150). The theme of aging and obsolescence is, of course, in no way implied in the traditional story of Salome (Mallarmé's Hérodiade) and Saint John. The many Salomes of late 19th-century literature tend to project a death wish on their part or on the part of their beholders, but Mallarmé's Hérodiade does not exist on the plane of the living: "Un baiser me tûrait / Si la beauté n'était la mort." At the same time, Hérodiade and her sunken, fateful land are never annihilated, never truly abolished in death, but perpetually tend towards Nothingness.

The peculiar mode of Being and Non-being which we find in Hérodiade's person and background would seem related to the experience of Nothingness Mallarmé alludes to in his letters. He remained physically alive, but was no longer "the Stéphane you knew." Nothingness was not annihilation in the crudest sense, but an otherness compared with the will to life. For an analogue, worked out with the help of esoteric theology, we can point to Yeat's fifteenth phase of the moon in "Byzantium," where the soul has become a work of art, the "superhuman," indifferently called "death-in-life" or "life-in-death." The paradox of a living poet having experienced Nothingness inevitably calls forth these complicated intermediates between the vulgar idea of life and death.

It would be perhaps supererogatory to demand of Mallarmé, in his verse and letters, a new theoretical vocabulary to cover his experience. As a result, we find him using the Christian mythology of his education, where death and rebirth occur in a spiritual sense on earth, as well as in a more concrete sense. When he had discovered the secret of the poem he had been working at for a year and a half, Mallarmé felt his mind was moving in "eternity" (I, 216) and that he had been "reborn" after the deathly experience of Nothingness (I, 222). Life in death, death in life, death of the old Adam, and rebirth in annihilation are a powerfully and ambiguously suggestive group of Christian notions, however much Mallarmé had dissoci-ated himself from God and religion by this time. Of course, these concep-tions could, after the mid-19th century, take on an oriental flavor, and we find Mallarmé comparing himself to the sacred spider of Indian thought, the great cosmological symbol which stands for unity, since the spider draws the substance of its web from within itself. However, in the guise of spiritual rebirth into eternity or of the great spider, the basic philosoph-ical step is the same: the anguish of dualism and unresolvable antithesis was at an end for Mallarmé.

II

With the overcoming of dualistic thinking, there is great enthusiasm and excitement in Mallarmé's letters from mid-1866 on, contrasting with his depression of 1865. He has found the basis of his life's work (I, 222), his secret. The image of the spider or keystone represents wholeness, an imper-sonal wholeness, he feels in his mind. Poems will be points of intersection in the spiderweb (I, 225). He speaks of the five volumes he is planning, which suggests some great system (I, 225).

Mallarmé also speaks of studying philosophy (I, 226). After a visit from the "very Hegelian" Lefébure in the summer of 1866 (I, 222n), Mallarmé received a letter from Villiers de l'Isle-Adam, famous for his Hegelianism, complimenting Mallarmé on devoting attention to the German philosopher (I, 231n). The creative use Mallarmé made of certain elements of Hegel's philosophy is the decisive orientation in his intellectual life—and one that continued to prove fruitful in Mallarmé's later years. The role of oral trans-mission, articles, or translations in Mallarmé's absorption of certain Hegel-ian notions is not a problem that allows any clear solution.[5] However, it would seem that Mallarmé's source is ultimately Hegel's *Encyclopedia of Philosophical Sciences*, especially certain key sections in "The Science of Logic," perhaps the beginning of "The Philosophy of Nature," and proba-bly the end of "The Philosophy of Mind." These areas of Hegel's work offer ideas which can be transplanted and recombined, the process that accounts for the varied manifestations of Hegel's influence in general on Western thought.

The basic tendencies of Hegel's philosophy were also in harmony with Mallarmé's attitudes, beyond any specific concept. To begin with, Hegel sought not a description of empirical reality, but what he called truth: the result of dialectic and his peculiar "science of logic." Dualisms were an abhorrence to him, and his method consists of finding comprehensive formulations in which dualisms disappear or are *aufgehoben*, which means raised to a higher level, synthesized, reconciled, and canceled all at once. Hegel's science of logic is a linguistic discipline, and linguistic and intellectual coherence takes precedence over the dualisms of vulgar reason. For example, the most famous triadic formulation in Hegel is the synthesis of Being and Nothingness in the idea of Becoming (and not in the Absolute, as Mallarmé has it). Of this *Aufhebung* Hegel says: "It is just as necessary and true to distinguish them [Being and Nothingness] as it is to unite them as inseparable. . . . It does not require much wit to poke fun at the proposition that Being and Nothing are one. . . . Such thoughtless foolishness stems from practical utilitarian interests for which the existence and non-existence of a good thing is of vital importance" (pp. 104-05).[6] Nothing perhaps could have been more congenial to Mallarmé than this dismissal of the practical, which fits in perfectly with the whole polemic against the useful in French Romantic art-for-art's-sake thinking.

The impersonality Mallarmé felt his mind had achieved is discursively accounted for in Hegel: "*Subjective appropriation* and *objective content* are dialectical opposites in and of the Concept; it is thus at once 'subject-object.' Truth exists for itself in the Concept and nowhere else" (p. 133). Hegel's dialectic makes the passage from the individual to the universal perfectly logical in its own terms: "I am what we all are; we all are what I am. This is the *concrete universality* of the Concept. The dialectical meeting of I and thou unites the concrete identity and the concrete universality of the Concept in one and the same living universe of discourse" (p. 135). Mallarmé considered himself in a sense exemplary in that his revelation, to be made in his projected works, would necessarily carry conviction. There is little thought of himself at this time as a *poète maudit,* scorned by society. Rather, it is the sense of elation derived from the powers of language which overcomes him. Hegel's thought seems to await a poet as linguistically oriented as Mallarmé, who can see the world as discourse. Moreover, "Language is both subjective and objective. It is the objective medium in which subjective minds meet" (p. 226). Language, truth, the Concept, and the poet's mind all seem to fuse together in the realm beyond any empirical concerns.

Of the Concept Mallarmé said, with the usual emotive coloring thought took on for him in the crisis of 1866-1868: "I have just spent a frightening year: my Thought thought itself and reached a pure Conception" (I, 240). This was written one year after the beginning of the crisis and its "Buddhist" phase in the spring of 1866. The reflexive formulation is characteristic of Hegel: "The *Concept* of philosophy is truth knowing itself, the idea thinking itself, the spirit living its thought" (pp. 285-86); "As Concept, reality becomes conscious of itself in the thinking mind" (p. 85). The word *concept* refers less to a content than to a movement of thought, for the drama of the mind in Hegel is partly one of self-consciousness. One of the most valuable aspects of Hegel's philosophy lies precisely in distinguishing the activity of thought from specific cases of it. Even when he alludes to particular thoughts, Hegel often prefers formulas which emphasize structures rather than detail: "*Forms* or shapes of the Concept, woven into a living spiritual texture, constitute reality" (p. 133). This reality, like that of the "living universe of discourse" alluded to above, is in no wise other-worldly, for a distinction between the this-worldly and the beyond, like that between subjectivity and objectivity, is not allowed to persist in the synthesizing movement of Hegelian dialectic. Again we see how relevant to the poetic mind Hegel's thought is and how the primacy of language, identified with the Concept, is affirmed over and over again.

Certain other terms occur in Hegel and Mallarmé as the final form of thought is envisaged. "The Absolute is present in the subject thinking it" (p. 84), and "the Absolute is Idea" (p. 152). Hegel is, as usual, more interested in the structure of thought than in questions of content; the Absolute was godhead for him, but his philosophy permits other interpretations than a German Protestant one, for "the Absolute Idea is not the idea *of* something or other; rather it differentiates itself into many concrete systems of life and remains the One all-embracing process and activity in all of them" (p. 153). The concept of a totality of the process of thought—which is also the cosmic totality—is taken up by Mallarmé, for whom it is the "Idea of the Universe," which he arrived at "by sensation alone" (I, 259). Mallarmé was, as we see, conscious of his more poetic than philosophical point of view, which allowed him to make an original recreation of Hegel's movement of the mind. "I must undergo the developments of thought necessary for the universe to find in me its identity" (I, 242). The poetic coloring shows up not only in the suggestions of the concrete in Mallarmé's "Idea of the Universe," but also in the fact that "Beauty by man's philosophical science is correlated in all its phases with the Universe" (I, 246). This bold identification of the thought process and the poem expresses nicely the original nuance by which we see that Mallarmé's direction of reasoning is at once distinct from and analogous to that of Hegel. Whereas for the latter, there were differences among religion, art, and philosophy, Mallarmé conflates the three as he envisages a totally new kind of poetry. When Hegel remarks that "Beauty is absolute spirit sensible" (p. 270), we perceive some ghost of a dualism between the sensible and the abstract forms of spirit, but Mallarmé obviates any such dichotomy by the fact that poetry is for him not simply sensible, but is itself the all-embracing Idea. The fact that Mallarmé conceives of a synchronic idea, rather than one working itself out in history, as Hegel does, need not bother us; it is one of the fruitful ambiguities of Hegel's thought that we may read the universal process in more than one way.

The Hegelian spirit is very evident not only in the letters, but also in some notes Mallarmé made on language in 1869. Philosophical method is a "fiction" in the positive sense of something created, and the instrument of this fiction is language (851).[7] The term *Science* is used in Hegelian fashion to denote the special logic of the German philosopher: "Science, having found in language a confirmation of itself, must now become a confirmation of language" (852). The paradoxical formulation is highly Hegelian, and Mallarmé goes on to indicate that one of the duties of science is to "discover what spirit is in relation to its double expression, matter and humanity, and how our world is connected to the Absolute" (853). Mallarmé's "science" is comprehensible only as the movement of dialectic inquiry, and its objects are the Hegelian ones of Being and Nothingness and the Absolute. Furthermore, Mallarmé notes that "pure science" comes from Germany.

III

At the end, in 1868, of what Mallarmé regarded as the two-year philosophical crisis, he concluded that his vast plans for works were impracticable and that he would resign himself to writing poems merely "tinged" with the Absolute, which is perhaps a way of stating the equivalent of Hegel's notion that in art, philosophy sees the counterpart of its own Concept in intuitive and mythical symbols (p. 285). The Absolute is not expressed directly in art. In any case, the "sonnet in -yx" ("Ses purs ongles" in its final form) is the immediate poetic result (1868) of the two years of theorizing, which saw plans for works, but no actual poetry, it would appear. The intellectual background and implications of the sonnet in -yx permit us an initial appreciation of what Mallarmé's version of obviously Hegelian notions meant in esthetic terms.

One of the curious developments Mallarmé made of the distinction between Being and Nothingness is that the latter is identified with chance and with dream in the pejorative sense of *rêvasserie* or *Träumerei*; it is vagueness and indefinition. For Hegel, on the other hand, Nothingness could be seen as a form of freedom, but the general notion of freedom, so important for the German philosopher, has no relevance to Mallarmé's thought. Rather, he saw the highest good in the imposition of structure, the abolition of chance, and for Mallarmé, doubtless, what he gleaned of Hegel's philosophy represented a very remarkable example of creating linguistic order out of the vagueness of life and experience. Hegel's imposition of form, finally, can be identified with Mallarmé's earlier stylistic theory, which could be summed up as composition or the relevance of the parts to the whole. On a vast scale, Hegel's philosophy attempts to relate all of knowledge not through catalogues, but by the discovery of logical articulations. In Mallarmé's commentary, in a letter, on the sonnet in -yx, he insists at once on the way the words and parts of the sonnet stylistically "reflect one another" and on the thematic cohesion, which involves an "incomprehensible" glow in a mirror appearing as the answer to a "night made of absence and questioning" (I, 278-79). Form in style and thought merge, for "Concepts of philosophy are concrete realities, thought together with their opposites" (p. 84).

The concepts of the poem are initially Being (light, the sun, which has disappeared) and Nothingness:

> Ses purs ongles très haut dédiant leur onyx,
> L'Angoisse, ce minuit, soutient, lampadophore,
> Maint rêve vespéral brûlé par le Phénix
> Que ne recueille pas de cinéraire amphore
>
> Sur les crédences, au salon vide: nul ptyx,
> Aboli bibelot d'inanité sonore,
> (Car le Maître est allé puiser des pleurs au Styx
> Avec ce seul objet dont le Néant s'honore).

(In an act of consecration, this midnight, the lamp-statue of Anguish raises high its pure black fingernails, as if supporting the ashen remains of many an evening dream burnt up by the Phoenix of the sunset and not gathered in any funereal urn. On the sideboards, in the empty salon, there is no ptyx, a suppressed knick-knack in which emptiness echoes—for the Master has gone to seek tears from the Styx with this object, which, alone, Nothingness will recognize.)

(This later version of the poem reinforces with greater stylistic deftness the original pattern; Mallarmé's thought is consistent, but underwent a process of broadening and deepening.) The passage from Being into Nothingness is one of Mallarmé's most original variations on Hegel's thought. When the latter speaks of Being and Nothingness, he usually has, in the back of his mind, the old theological notion of creation *ex nihilo*, and he is concerned with the movement from Nothing to Being, not the other way round. Mallarmé, however, had experienced the concepts as a process in which vulgar reality ceases to have any consistency and the mind faces pure vacuity. Thus his imagery is made ghostly by the dim suggestion of a black lamp with a figure as its base, a statue-lamp, which then is seen as *not being* an amphora gathering the remains of a dream in light. ("Dream" here has the positive sense it often has in Mallarmé and which must be sharply distinguished from the shapeless, idle, chance images designated by "dream" on other occasions.) Stylistic detail—the shadowy periphrases and images of the absent—becomes identified with conceptual values.

"No art," says Hegel, "imitates nature except accidentally; it seeks the spiritual sense of phenomena" (p. 272). We might add that when a poet attempts to express the Idea of the Universe, he need not use images of the conventionally beautiful. In the course of Mallarmé's letters from 1866 to 1868, we discern a growing concern with the Absolute as totality and a decrease in the insistence on the idea of beauty, which is too suggestive of the estheticizing Parnassian ideal of imagery. The furniture of "Ses purs ongles" demonstrates perfectly the passage from estheticizing to philosophically symbolic imagery.

The poem concludes in an indirect or reflected vision of light, conveying the half-glimpsed Absolute:

> Mais proche la croisée au nord vacante, un or
> Agonise selon peut-être le décor
> Des licornes ruant du feu contre une nixe,
>
> Elle, défunte nue en le miroir, encor
> Que, dans l'oubli fermé par le cadre, se fixe
> De scintillations sitôt le septuor.

(But near the window opening onto the north, there is dying gold light, perhaps from the representation in relief, on the frame of a mirror, of unicorns throwing fire at a watersprite. The image of the naked sprite has vanished in the mirror, although, in the oblivion the frame encloses, soon there will be fixed the seven sparkling stars of the Big Dipper.)

The Absolute is represented by light, but a different light from that of the sun, as suits the passage of Being through a dialectic: "If this mutual alienation is comprehended, Being negates its negation and thereby affirms itself as the one in the other. It then remains itself in all changes and transitions. This is *true infinity* of Being" (p. 107). The infinity of the night sky with stars is the higher vision of Being. The whole poem constitutes the Idea or Mallarmé's Idea of the Universe, which is not only the endpoint, but the totality of processes by which the Absolute is reached. The formal or stylistic order of the poem is identical in all its detail with the dialectic or order of the universe. (The image of the sprite and unicorns belongs also to this pattern, but we must postpone, for the moment, the discussion of this important side of Mallarmé's symbolism.) Naturally the rising gaze associated with starlight, as well as the Christian symbolism of the star, inclines us to see in the image some notion of hope or succor—which is perfectly consonant with Hegel's very positive tone. Nothingness (*néant*) has, on the other hand, a strong theological aura in French: going back to Descartes, we find the term designates non-God, the shadow of spiritual and physical emptiness.

The fact that "Ses purs ongles" is a more intense version of a sonnet of 1868 ("La nuit approbatrice")—but strictly in the same thematic gamut—suggests that another sonnet published in the 1880s, "Quand l'ombre menaça," might have similar early origins, for its imagery and structure have strong analogies with the first and ultimate forms of "Ses purs ongles." The moment after sunset is alluded to in the first quatrain:

> Quand l'ombre menaça de la fatale loi
> Tel vieux Rêve, désir et mal de mes vertèbres,
> Affligé de périr sous les plafonds funèbres
> Il a ployé son aile indubitable en moi.

(When, with its fateful regularity, the shadow of night threatened some old dream, which is like a painful desire at the back of my neck, my dream like a bird, desolate at dying under the funereal ceiling of night, folded in me its wings, real and suffering.)

The "fatal law" is both the alternation of day and darkness and the disappearance of Being into Nothingness. These lines correspond to Mallarmé's definition of tragedy which he formulated in regard to *Hamlet*: the antagonism between dream, in its positive sense, and the fatalities weighing on mankind. The dying stars of the night sky are apostrophized in terms that recall the Glorious Lie of apparent Being, as Mallarmé had expressed it in his "Buddhist" phase:

> Vous n'êtes qu'un orgueil menti par les ténèbres
> Aux yeux du solitaire ébloui de sa foi.

(You are only a lie, the false pride of the shadow, in the eyes of the solitary poet dazzled by his faith in his art.)

The reflexive character of the solitary man's self-illumination is made more precise at the end of the poem:

> L'espace à soi pareil qu'il s'accroisse ou se nie
> Roule dans cet ennui des feux vils pour témoins
> Que s'est d'un astre en fête allumé le génie.

(Space, always the same whether its existence is magnified or denied, rolls wearily with its vile stars, bearing witness that the genius of a festive planet has lit up.)

Space—often a pejorative term in Mallarmé, suggesting a kind of insecurity of the individual—can, as Being, be affirmed, or, as all Being passes into Nothingness, be denied any existence. In any case, the self-nourishment of the genius or poet casting his own light symbolizes the reflexive turn of thought ("my Thought thought itself") when it arrives at the pure Concept. The movement differs from the one at the end of "Ses purs ongles" in that the poet becomes the concrete universal, as is represented by his self-affirmation before the cosmos. The notion of man's relation to the universe will become more and more a theoretical concern for Mallarmé.

In a poet whose physical and emotional states were so bound up in his thought processes, it would not be surprising to find that the "moments of synthesis" are complemented by a certain tendency to relapse into discouragement and dualism. Mallarmé's friend Lefébure warned him in 1867 that he was still a prey to "our ugly and inborn antithesis" (I, 247n), while Mallarmé was insisting that one should think with both mind and body. A sonnet whose first version dates from 1868 brings out strongly, in its second form (written in the early 1870s, it would seem),[8] the sense of anguish which Being, as much as Nothingness, can provoke:

> De l'oubli magique venue,
> Nulle étoffe, musique et temps,
> Ne vaut la chevelure nue
> Que, loin des bijoux, tu détends.
>
> En mon rêve, antique avenue
> De tentures, seul, si j'entends
> Le Néant, cette chère nue
> Enfouira mes yeux contents!

(No fabric handed down from the magic past and evoking music and time can match the naked hair which, free of jewels, you stretch out. In my dream, which is an avenue of ancient hangings, if, alone, I should hear Nothingness, the dear cloud of your hair will bury my happy eyes.)

We see, in the association of rich artifacts from the past and of menacing Nothingness, an echo of the imagery of Hérodiade's manor. At first the human seems to be a refuge from disintegration. (The image of a woman's hair, we should note, antedated Mallarmé's affair with Méry Laurent, so that the poems in which her hair is celebrated merely represent a further version of an old theme.) The curious thing about this sonnet, which begins like one of the late love poems, is that, in the reversal constituted by the tercets, there is no synthesis or *Aufhebung*, but rather a sense of ghastliness:

> Non. Comme par les rideaux vagues
> Se heurtent du vide les vagues,
> Pour un fantôme les cheveux
>
> Font luxueusement renaître
> La lueur parjure de l'Etre,
> Son horreur et ses désaveux.

(It will not be so. As the waves of emptiness make the moving curtains writhe, your hair, for the ghost that I am, gives a luxurious rebirth to the mendacious glow of Being, its horror and disavowals.)

The poet, deprived of his own substance, experiences the instability of Being, after the ancient hangings—perhaps brocades, with a texture heavy with Being—yield to the head of hair, as to something more affirmative. *Rêve* and physicality are both undone in this apprehension of Nothingness.

Mallarmé's peculiar state of mind as his great synthesis threatened to dissolve was most elaborately put forth in the philosophical tale *Igitur* (1869), which, though unfinished and never published by Mallarmé, allows one clearly to see the metaphysical formulations that disturbed its author. The experience of Nothingness, banished in the moments of synthesis, returns in an insidious form in *Igitur*. However, we must not take the tale as necessarily having a negative sense in the development of Mallarmé's thought, for he spoke of it as a homeopathic remedy ("similia similibus," I, 313) for the inability to write and create. Too simplistic a reading of *Igitur* gives the totally false idea of it as representing "catastrophe" in Mallarmé's life; such an interpretation ignores the pointed humor of the whole strange work. Exorcism was the function of *Igitur* in Mallarmé's œuvre.

Igitur concerns the last survivor of a great family, on whom is incumbent an act—represented as blowing out a candle or casting dice—which will cancel chance, the infinite, and immortality in favor of the Absolute. In other words, the realms of Being and Nothingness (dominated by chance and indefiniteness) and of Christian myth are suppressed by an act of symbolic import. The casting of dice negates chance by chance: a double negative produces a positive result. The alternative act of blowing out the candle is the extinction of the universe, the domain of chance and infinity in a negative sense. The acts are, of course, absurd, but Igitur's race, having suffered from the "old space" of heaven, has passed on the ancestral summons to try, in the end, recourses which seem to have no meaning.

In the section called "Midnight," Igitur contemplates a room in his manor, before going down to the ancestral tombs to accomplish the act. The imagery is related to that of "Ses purs ongles":

The hour has not disappeared in a mirror, has not fled into the hangings.... I remember that its golden light was, in the midst of absence, about to feign an elusive dream jewel, a rich and useless survival—except that on goldwork, like starlight or reflections on the sea, the infinite chance of combinations could be read.

But in this revelation of midnight, it has never up to now indicated such a juncture, for this now is the only hour it has created, and from infinity the sea and constellations have been separated—although seemingly they are Nothingness—in order that their essence, in this moment of union, create the Absolute Presence of things.

Here we have a discursive presentation of the "incomprehensible" starlight and golden reflections of "Ses purs ongles." Mallarmé complements his philosophical vocabulary with the theological term "Presence," containing a Eucharistic reference and allusion to the mystery of the mass. (Liturgical vessels are perhaps implied by "goldwork.") However, the jewel is qualified as fleeting or "nul," which could mean that it both is and is not, that is, lies beyond Being and Nothingness, or else that the Absolute Presence is elusive. In fact, negative words seem to be the only ones adequate for this hour, the only one created:

It is the pure dream of a Midnight disappeared into itself, and whose recognizable brightness (remaining alone in the midst of the shadow of its coming about) exemplifies its sterility on the pale page of an open book on the table.

The book, a *grimoire*, or book of magic, is associated with the "silent" ancestral prediction and summons. The passage from the idea of purity to that of sterility indicates a subtle change of connotations. Igitur, in this unique hour, is to be made "pure" or Absolute, but his act or gesture will be empty:

The ancient idea—long dead—of the prediction gleams in the fantastic gold figure, where its Dream writhed in death. It can be recognized in the empty and immemorial gesture by which, to end this polar antagonism, it reaches the averted chaos of shadow and the words which have made Midnight Absolute.

Useless . . . the hour . . . .

To purity, sterility, and emptiness is now joined the idea of "uselessness." The ambiguity of the Absolute is further suggested when Igitur is about to leave the room and "get lost on the stairs (instead of sliding down the banister)":

The time for me to leave has come; the purity of the mirror will exist without that character, that vision of me, but that character will take off the light, the night! On the empty furniture Dream has agonized in the glass vial—purity—which contains the substance of Nothingness.

I think we are meant to see the vial of purity in two different perspectives: by containing Nothingness it puts an end to the chance oscillation of Being and Nothingness, or else purity turns out in the end to be merely Nothingness. Mallarmé's concern with the pure and the self-reflexive can therefore appear as a more self-destructive than self-creative movement of thought. Ambiguity is, however, the method of *Igitur,* the ambiguity implied in the idea of the necessary yet absurd.

Igitur's madness is admitted in the penultimate section, "The Cast of the Dice," and to emphasize it, Mallarmé prefaces his disquisition on the dice throw with the absurd tautology, "Le Cornet est la Corne de licorne —d'unicorne." Mallarmé's logic has a secret coherence beneath its surface like the Aristotelian formulas concealed in the old jargon of "barbara and baralipton." "Le Cornet est la Corne" constitutes a precaution that we may take all that follows as having a purely linguistic existence and make of it what we will. Igitur assumes his folly, admits the cast of the dice, and takes on himself the Idea, or conception of the universe from the perspective of the Absolute. Since he has willed his assumption of the Idea and Act, which deny chance, he concludes that the Idea, like the Act, is necessary. To will, on the part of one absorbed into the Absolute, becomes the concrete universal of necessity. If through madness chance is denied, madness also is necessary: "For what? (No one knows; he [Igitur] is isolated from humanity.)" "You can see what the ambiguity of his act means."

All the section on casting the dice may be seen not only as a symbolic commentary on Mallarmé's creation of a metaphysics in 1866-1868 drawn from some Hegelian notions, but also as commentary on the tortuous process by which he achieved the Idea. Mallarmé was aware of a certain precariousness in his "moments of synthesis" and of the strong emotive and physical basis of his thought. This does not mean, however, that he abandoned his position of the late 1860s. Rather, one might say that he left such notions in abeyance for a time while other intellectual constructs presented themselves to him as more demanding of attention. But the old Idea, the Absolute, was not abandoned, for it still promised a special kind of poetry understood by no one so well as Mallarmé. At the end of *Igitur,* after the protagonist has evidently committed suicide by drinking the drop of Nothingness in the glass vial, "there remained the castle of purity," or the poem.

Chapter V

MALLARMÉ'S LATER WORK

Nothing in his earlier work prepares us to encounter, in Mallarmé's correspondence of the 1870s, mention of a *drame populaire* or melodrama he is working on (e.g., II, 94, 103). Gradually this becomes an entirely new theatrical entertainment, magic, proletarian, and partly sung (II, 151). The poet is in isolation preparing his œuvre (II, 153), a word which always suggests something of great scope in Mallarmé. There is talk of dazzling "the sovereign populace" with his new form of theater (II, 159). This interest in the proletarian anticipates certain sides of Symbolist taste epitomized by Des Esseintes's preference, in landscapes, for the desolate areas outside the Paris fortifications, where the working class took walks. Mallarmé had already written about the popular *orgue de Barbarie* (in "Plainte d'automne"), and two other prose poems have lower-class subjects ("Réminiscence" and "Pauvre Tête pâle" in their final titles). *L'Assommoir,* not surprisingly, moved Mallarmé far more than Zola's previous fiction. However, using popular subjects and writing in a popular genre are rather different. The late anecdote "Conflit" (*Variations sur un sujet,* 1895) is more in the Symbolist manner: the poet listens to workmen with their intrusive noise as they dig a ditch, and wonders if they are conscious of the cosmic drama of sunset when they drink and lie on "Mother Earth."

Cosmic drama is, in fact, what Mallarmé begins to write about in his prose pieces of the 1880s, as his very unusual project of a *drame populaire* is gradually abandoned. Mallarmé actually described once a melodrama which appears to be more his dream of melodrama than anything to be found on the French stage: its subject is Man's Passion, underscored by music, with its indispensable mystery (296-97). But before pursuing further the subject matter of the new dramatic texts Mallarmé began to envision, we had best examine Mallarmé's speculations on a new mode of theatrical representation and its physical character.

It is essential to emphasize Mallarmé's very modern idea of play when we approach his conception of theater: one plays music, games, and theatrical pieces; the form-giving idea is the essential one, the creation of pattern where before there was only raw life. Mallarmé defines poetry as a game (647)—as did T.S. Eliot, moreover—and when we sense that side of the work of art, its potential connection with an ideal, stylized drama becomes evident. The poem is even play in its origins: the writer writing creates a space, a stage around himself, and the specific content of this play is that the poet, by self-sacrifice, is reborn as an impersonal artist (370). The page separates the completed poem from banality (334), that is, from Being and Nothingness. The cosmos emanates from the poem (334) and forms its natural space. The Figure (a term Mallarmé prefers for the single actor) makes gestures which are the rhythms of an ideal, unheard music (545); the other element necessary to theater is the gaze of the audience, whose cynosure the Figure constitutes (545).

It should be obvious by now that the archetype of Mallarmé's theater is the mass with its representation of Christ's self-sacrifice and our redemption. The notion of play coincides with that of ritual for Mallarmé. There is an intricate tradition of commentary on the mass as symbolic performance,[1] which Mallarmé may have known through his fairly extensive religious education; and, moreover, French scholars had widely disseminated their findings on the ritual origins of theater and on the dramatic character of the mass.[2] These notions gave an entirely new potential perspective on the nature of the theater, making it appear at once far more serious than the plays of the 19th century and reducing its essential traits to a minimum. It would seem, actually, from refutations of the school of theorists of drama as myth and ritual that such ideas reflected less the facts of Greek or other early theater than they prepared the way for a new kind of dramaturgy in the 20th century, which Mallarmé anticipated.[3] For Mallarmé was in the vanguard of a new thinking; his conception of drama remained unsurpassed for its clarity and daring until well into the 20th century. In the English-speaking world after 1910, Gilbert Murray's studies in Greek tragedy spread the conception of drama as ritual which is embodied in such a modern book as Francis Fergusson's *The Idea of Theater* (1949) and is now widely alluded to in works on dramatic art. In France, the ritual conception of drama is particularly associated with Jean Genet. Such views of theater, in their most thorough-going form, are relatively recent, which makes Mallarmé's theorizing all the more strikingly prophetic: he bypassed the whole Symbolist drama movement to formulate a radical, essential notion of the play as forming the core of religious experience and the organizing principle of society.

Advanced thinking about theater has almost always been accompanied by a new consciousness of society—often taking extremely dogmatic forms.[4] Like others after him, Mallarmé saw theater as the Holy of Holies (134); it

would be the center of a utopia of justice (545). The highest glory would
be the creation, through art, of a new idol or religious art for a delirious
people (II, 264). If a new religion were to arise, it would consist of a ritual
hymn, perhaps closing some cycle of history, through which all would be
reborn (335-36, 645). Mallarmé emerged from the negative *l'art pour l'art*
social thought of his youth with the help of his new idea of theater. The
notion of social cohesion implied in Mallarmé's conception of drama puts
it at a great remove from the usual Symbolist emphasis on an elite. But his
new drama has a specific content, without which it would be pointless.

One facet of the content of ideal theater is nature with its cyclical movement: the theater of nature in autumn (299) or the theater of clouds and
sunset (299); the fable inscribed on the page of the sky (544-45), which is
the only myth and present in us all; the background of sky and ecstacy or
thunder on the page of a book, which is "our essence" (334); the tragedy
of nature and tetralogy of the year (1169). No stage is needed; the con-
templator of nature supplies the theatrical situation (328, 315). However,
nature is not seen in its otherness, to use a Hegelian expression, but in
relation to ourselves; poetry should contain "the play written on the folio
of the sky and acted by Man, with the gestures of his Passions" (249).
The Absolute, mind, and nature mediate one another, according to Hegel
(p. 286), or, to put it differently, nature and spirit are double aspects of a
concrete totality (p. 287).

Mallarmé also speaks of Man's Passion in the singular (296), as well as
of the tragedy of nature, and it is worth pausing over the expression to
examine its implications. The tradition of symbolic commentary on the
mass held it to be a repetition of Christ's life in which we participate, and
Mallarmé's idea of a collective rebirth from theater certainly stresses the
salvational character of his ideal ceremony. What seems to be specifically
implied in Man's Passion is the undergoing of a tragic experience followed
by a psychological resurrection. The tragedy is human aspiration, which
is correlated with the solar drama: the sun is the heroic, victorious symbol
at whose setting man senses the disparity between dreams of glory and his
condemnation to the cycle of Being and Nothingness. The "tetralogy of
the year" is a larger cyclic form and one found in the mass, where from
Advent to All Souls' Day an annual drama takes place. Salvation for Mallarmé takes the form of a release from cyclic bondage and is expressed
by nocturnal light, in contrast to the day cycle, and would presumably
find some appropriate symbol with respect to the progress of the year.
"Ses purs ongles" is the nucleus of a myth of tragedy and rebirth, with
its doomed Master seeking the Styx and the image of celestial light which
terminates it. The poem is a miniature symbolic play.

The significance of the solar drama seems to have been reinforced in Mallarmé's mind by the study of the writings of the English scholar George Cox, whom he translated.[5] Cox was not the important ethnologist his more famous contemporary and compatriot E.B. Taylor was, but his singlemind-ed thesis proved of great value to Mallarmé. Cox believed that all religious phenomena could be traced to the sun cult, just as later reductivists posited the fertility cult or some other such primitive ritual as the basis for the development of myths. Like the anthropology behind *The Waste Land,* Cox's theory of comparative religion now appears most important for the poetry it inspired. It gave Mallarmé what seemed an objective and even scientific grounding for his solar drama, just as the new notions of ritual as the historical basis of theater formed a scholarly background for his dramatic ideas. Mallarmé's thinking has analogues and justification in the research of his own century.

"Our dreams of sites or paradises" are another essential part of the cosmic theater (545), and here we see Mallarmé's old myth of the original state of unity recur. Now, however, paradise has a decidedly ahistorical sense and is not accompanied by any notion of a Fall. It is relevant to look briefly at two rather ceremonious poems in order to see how, in verse only "tinged" with the Absolute, Mallarmé's feelings about "man's authentic earthly dwelling place" (545) find expression. The first poem is the "Toast funèbre" for Théophile Gautier, which opens with a long rhetorical evoca-tion of death and ghosts, of Being passing into Nothingness. In contrast, Eden is described:

> Le Maître, par un œil profond, a, sur ses pas,
> Apaisé de l'Eden l'inquiète merveille
> Dont le frisson final, dans sa voix seule, éveille
> Pour la Rose et le Lys le mystère d'un nom.

(The Master has, with his deep gaze, quieted the quivering marvel of Eden, whose final shudder evokes in his voice alone the mystery of a name for the rose and lily.)

Mallarmé is here describing the ritual of paradise rather than the Passion of Man against the background of the natural cycle. The act of naming is either pseudo-historical and represents the origin of mind and language or synchronic and refers to each poet's realizing his vocation. Whereas the passive submission to Being and Nothingness is the fate of most men, the poet creates the Absolute, and we see

> A qui s'évanouit, hier, dans le devoir
> Idéal que nous font les jardins de cet astre,
> Survivre pour l'honneur du tranquille désastre
> Une agitation solenelle par l'air

De paroles, pourpre ivre et grand calice clair,
Que, pluie et diamant, le regard diaphane
Resté là sur ces fleurs dont nulle ne se fane,
Isole parmi l'heure et le rayon du jour!

(Something survive of him who vanished yesterday pursuing the ideal duty of the gardens of this planet, someting survive like a solemn agitation of words in the air, words like drunken purple and a great pale flower, which his gaze, bright as rain or diamonds, isolates amid the hour and daylight, as it lingers on flowers of which none ever fades.)

Making words, the stuff of the Idea, is the poet's duty and the only real "occupation of our paradise." In contrast to Igitur's absurd method of attempting to reach the Absolute through casting dice or blowing out a candle, the poet makes language, which is the "living spiritual texture" of reality, as Hegel puts it. The poem concludes with the image of darkness and silence shut up in the tomb: Nothingness is contained, fixed, and circumscribed, as in the "aboli bibelot d'inanité sonore" ("Ses purs ongles") or in the vial Igitur drinks from.

Mallarmé's *tombeaux* tend to reflect some facet of the poet evoked like the bright visual images of language in the "Toast funèbre" for Gautier. Something similar occurs in "Prose pour des Esseintes," where, from the medieval liturgical term used as title through the exotically colored Christian references, we find a poem suited to its dedicatee. Mallarmé begins with suggestions of a rite:

Hyperbole! de ma mémoire
Triomphalement ne sais-tu
Te lever, aujourd'hui grimoire
Dans un livre de fer vêtu:

Car j'installe, par la science,
L'hymne des cœurs spirituels
En l'œuvre de ma patience,
Atlas, herbiers et rituels.

(Hyperbole! can you not rise triumphantly from my memory, now that you are a book of magic with iron clasps? For I install, through wisdom, the hymn of spiritual hearts in the work of my patience: atlases, herbals, and rituals.)

The poem is a commemoration like the mass, and an elevation ("te lever") coming from the proper use of the sacred text or *grimoire* is its purpose. The hyperbole or preternatural miracle will repeat the sacred experience in the paradise-island:

Oui, dans une île que l'air charge
De vue et non de visions
Toute fleur s'étalait plus large

Sans que nous en devisions.

· · · · · · ·

Gloire du long désir, Idées
Tout en moi s'exaltait de voir
La famille des iridées
Surgir à ce nouveau devoir.

(Yes, in an island whose air was heavy with sight—and not mere visions—all the flowers grew bigger without our saying a thing about it. . . . Glory of our long desire, Ideas! I was completely enraptured to see the iridaceae rise to this new duty.)

"Ideas" has here a Platonic and transcendent meaning suitable to the Christian convention of the poem. Since Mallarmé was not a philosopher in the normal sense, he could alter his vocabulary for the purpose of poetic effect without feeling any concern over logical discrepancies in his work.

The poet's companion, his Psyche, breaks the silence of the ceremony with the triumphant pseudo-liturgical Greek *Anástase!* ("Arise!") which marks the flower-poem's completion. After this elevation marking the height of the ritual, the verse concludes with a recollection of the empty tomb in Jerusalem. The companion has spoken,

Avant qu'un sépulcre ne rie
Sous aucun climat, son aïeul,
De porter ce nom: Pulchérie!
Caché par le trop grand glaïeul.

(Before a sepulcher could gape open in its ancestral land, ironically bearing the name Beauty! and half-hidden by some too huge gladiolus.)

The gladiolus represents the angel standing by the opening of the empty sepulcher, and this calm stanza constitutes the poem's "Ite, missa est," for the miracle and its commemoration are completed.

In this variant on his myth of poetic creation, Mallarmé focuses on the idea of *hyper*bole or *trans*cendence: the flowers are huge *beyond* reality, the material corpus of the poet's inspiration vanishes as the work of art rises *above* and *beyond* the tangible world. The poet's self-sacrifice (as in *Hérodiade*) and rebirth are ignored in order to insist on the miracle of the poem's origin and the further miracle that occurs as one devoutly reads it, for the ideal reader is one with the hieratic voice heard in the opening lines of "Prose pour des Esseintes." It is important to understand that the para-Christian elements in Mallarmé's thought, like the Hegelian ones, emerge in an intermittent fashion as he conceives of the basic shape of this or that poem or essay. Inconsistencies that would impair dogmatic philosophy are esthetic enrichments for his œuvre.

If we have no actual theatrical work from Mallarmé's hand in the 1870s and 1880s, ceremonial poems like "Toast funèbre" and "Prose pour des

Esseintes" usefully complement his essays on drama and allow us some glimpse into the ritualizing side of his imagination. With these in mind, and the perspective we have also gained from Mallarmé's theoretical writing on drama, we are now prepared better to understand his remarks on the actual theater of his day. Mallarmé held essentially that the non-musical theater of the time was an "interregnum" in art (314), with the exception perhaps of stylized forms like farce (317) and mime (310). The peculiarity of modern theater is that nothing happens in it (296), which means that it is not based on a metaphysical event. It merely commands one to believe (542) instead of drawing one into worship. The theater with its realistic scenery is assimilated to the salon (314-15), and the audience unconsciously resents the sacrilege. For the public of Mallarmé's day still hungers for real theater and is frustrated by the "social arrangement" that deprives people of it (294). The social pact has been broken when true theater, the binding element in society, no longer exists (314). In such a situation the masses, without their natural theatrical nourishment, have an irregular, displaced position in society (314), and Mallarmé seems to find both bourgeois audiences and popular ones equally longing for an ideal theater. His sociology is based on the centrality in society of drama as worship and rebirth.

The Wagnerian cult of his day struck Mallarmé at best as having as object a temple only halfway up the sacred mount whose top is wreathed in clouds (545). Wagner represents a theoretically impossible fusion of decadent "personal" drama, that is, plays with realistically motivated human stories, and a vastly original form of music (543). The result appeared to Mallarmé at times as a mere juxtaposition (543), as the unfaithfulness of music to itself (335), or as the failure of the literary principle (542). Words implying vagueness and confused outlines describe Wagner's work (543-44). The significance of Mallarmé's "Rêverie" on Wagner becomes all the more important when one realizes that Mallarmé experienced the difficulty of never having seen a Wagner opera (II, 290). As on other occasions, however, a great deal of intuitive understanding reinforced a small amount of actual knowledge. Wagner's multiplication of myths struck Mallarmé as idle, for there is only *one* myth, that of rebirth or salvation against the background of nature. As a matter of fact, Wagner still had the kind of rationalistic conception of myth as readily translatable symbol which one finds in Creuzer's *Symbolik* (1810-1812) and which was retrograde with respect to the most imaginative Romantic literature.[6] The "personal" drama in Wagner is what all modern stagecraft since 1950 has been striving to eliminate: the horned helmets, clumsy naturalistic sets, and other devices which make us see Wagner as the prisoner of the theater of his day. As for music, Mallarmé's feeling that it was excessively loud and material has found its counterpart in modern attempts to reduce the volume of the *Ring* to a more chamber-like effect. Mallarmé's final contrast between Wagner and a hypothetical, totally "imaginative" and quintessential French art corresponds to the modern attempt to dematerialize Wagner's space and sound, making the operas into dramas of light rather than pseudo-reality. Wagner served Mallarmé to some extent as a foil, allowing him to epitomize his ideal drama, but in the course of his intuitive analysis of music drama, Mallarmé also proved to be prophetic.

Mallarmé was not less foresightful in his approach to dance. Although much of the ballet Mallarmé saw was the dreary, set-enclosed dancing by the graceless figures Degas painted and sculpted, he sensed that dance was potentially the highest form of pure poetry in the theater (308). How he arrived at the conception of the dancer as metaphor (304, 307) when watching the typical 19th-century French ballet—*Gisèle* is a fine example— is not entirely clear. He did intuit, however, that dance was a language, an ideal form of communication, which some creature beyond mortal powers could handle with expressive perfection (306-07). Actually, Mallarmé saw and admired one of the great inventors of modern dance, the American Loïe Fuller, whose abstract work is still impressive in the cinematographic record of it preserved. It was Loïe Fuller who led Mallarmé to the notion that physical theaters are meaningless, that the dancer *creates space* (307-09). The theorizers of modern dance have often developed this insight to the point that it is something of a commonplace, but again, Mallarmé seems, by his sense of form, to have been able to abstract from one brief example—comparable to his slight acquaintance with Wagner's music—a whole modernist esthetic.

II

It is impossible to separate Mallarmé's thought, from the mid-1880s on, from his reflections on music. While he had loved nature in his youth, he wrote in 1895, music had replaced it in age as an object of meditation (402). Both are forms of the sacred, but music, as more intellectual and abstract, now appealed to him especially. Music, he noted, provided the latest occasion for worship: the Sunday concert (new in Paris in the mid-1880s as a regular institution) took the place of Sunday mass (388, 393), and the fact that its audience was greater than that of poetry stimulated in part his cogitations.

Perhaps the most densely characteristic of his remarks about music is to be found in a letter to Edmund Gosse, where he refers to it "in the

Greek sense, meaning, basically, the Idea or a rhythm of relationships."[7] The Romantics had spoken of music in what they thought was a Greek sense when they used "harmony" to characterize a utopian society, but Mallarmé implies something quite different. It is clearly a succession of sounds rather than some one static total chord that he has in mind. The Pythagorean idea of mystic numbers doubtless was at the back of his mind, but the ordinary conception of the "harmony of the spheres" evidently was not, for it is too simplistic sounding in regard to any notion of structure. Mallarmé perhaps knew that Greek musical and poetic rhythms coincided, which would have been of great significance to him. The amount of second-hand knowledge he had of Greek music cannot be calculated easily; the oldest standard work on the subject dates from his lifetime,[8] but unquestionably the essentially slim practical acquaintance to be had of Hellenic music increased its prestige in his mind.

When we turn to the idea of music as relationships quite aside from any Greek antecedents, we come to the essential and most penetrating of Mallarmé's reflections. If we attempt to assess the significance of the new music, Wagner, on a listener of no particular musical culture, but of great intellectual curiosity, it seems likely that the new relational system in it would most clearly differentiate it from, say, the work of Gounod or other prominent French composers of Mallarmé's youth. Wagner often replaces melodic material, as it had been understood, with figures which are striking largely because they contain relations which had been forbidden in the most prominent parts of musical texture. To take a simple example, the death motif in *Tristan* consists of a major triad on A flat (inverted) followed by a major triad based on A natural. The chromaticism is not formed by voices in their evolving lines, but constitutes a stopping point, an overt harmonic clash by previous standards of composition. It is impossible not to be aware of an unusual relationship between the two triads; the ear cannot assimilate them to progressions so familiar as to be unnoticeable. This, I think, is the kind of musical fact which inspired Mallarmé's concept of a rhythm of relationships.

As with dance or the ritual conception of theater, Mallarmé's ideas on music have a certain prophetic value. The composer and theorist who was to develop most profoundly a theory of music as relationships was Arnold Schönberg, and the word occurs in significant parts of his treatise on harmony.[9] Like Mallarmé insisting on the system the words of a poem form in themselves, Schönberg eventually evolved a "method of composing with twelve tones which are related only with one another."[10] He rejected the distinction between consonances and dissonances—for him the basis of classical tonality—on the grounds that it was an extraneous, extra-musical notion. "Dissonances" are merely relationships that are difficult to under-

stand. Melody and harmony became based on the same intervals in his com-
positions of the 1920s and after, so that the interval was the whole *matière*
of music. This conception of unity and the rejection of any criticism based
on criteria of obscurity are also strongly implied in Mallarmé's stylistic
practice, and we discover that for him the essential structure of music, as
he saw it, differed little from that of poetry.

I have dealt with the more concrete, practical sense in which music consists of relationships, since for Mallarmé the latter are not entirely abstract:
his repeated definition of the poem as a reciprocal reflection of words
among themselves sufficiently indicates that the analogous art of music
is based on a similar structural principle. At the same time, however, the
notion of relationships has a far-reaching Hegelian sense for Mallarmé, and
music would seem, as much as poetry, to form a living, spiritual world of
discourse.

In a famous passage Mallarmé speaks of how poetry must "take back its
own from music," but he then proceeds to define music as "the intellectual
word at its apogee," which is profoundly ambiguous, for Mallarmé may be
slyly implying that poetry is, or should be, the true music. At the same
time, his frequent equation of the two makes such an interpretation only
a slight overtone. One of Mallarmé's several relational definitions (368,
378, 647, 648, 871) follows immediately: music and poetry contain "the
whole of relations existing among all things" (367-68). Such expressions
alternate in Mallarmé's late prose with succinct references to music and
poetry as "the Idea," "the evolving context of the Idea" (649, 653), with
which we might compare Hegel's statement that "the Absolute Idea is . . .
the One all-embracing process and activity." The network of relationships
found in the poem or piece of music stands for the universal system of
relationships: the individual work of art represents the whole. This transition from the specific to the most general is perfectly Hegelian in spirit
(for the universal is concrete), and indeed, Mallarmé's elaboration of concepts reminiscent of Hegel reaches its peak in the late essays: he no longer
defines the Idea as being that of the Universe, but follows the more elliptic Hegelian usage, according to which the Idea is so comprehensive it
cannot be said to be of anything. The totality of thought is the movement
of the whole through nature (the phenomenon) to spirit to the idea of
the whole or simply the Idea (p. 286). In this highest synthesis, Mallarmé
makes philosophy and art one, which is his own contribution to Hegelian
patterns of thought. Furthermore, in its perfect form the Idea as work of
art would also subsume religion.

As we reach such levels of theory, it becomes increasingly clear that
Mallarmé is not talking about any real piece of music or poetry, but about
the idea of art. One of the reasons he speaks of Greek music doubtless is to

divorce music from any known sounds, and when he refers to music as "the intellectual word at its apogee," he also specifically denies that it is a product of winds, strings, and brasses. The centrality of music to Mallarmé's esthetics comes from the fact that it is easier to imagine music in a theoretical form—as it appears, for example, written in a score—than it is to conceive of poetry as pure relationships. But it is abundantly clear that Mallarmé often means a soundless, hypothetical music (e.g., 334, 648), as when the Figure, or actor, makes gestures which are the silent rhythm of an ideal music accompanying Man's Passion (545).

In the late lecture, "La Musique et les lettres" (1894), one has the impression that the poetry invoked is also hypothetical, and this recourse to the pure idea of poetry is connected with one of the stranger facts of Mallarmé's career, the mass of notes now referred to as Le Livre.[11] In a number of places, but most overtly in the autobiographical account he wrote for Verlaine in 1885, Mallarmé spoke of the one book of which all books are variants. This Bible is the orphic explanation of the earth, and we see how Mallarmé's studies in comparative religion and philosophy support such a conception. To refer only to the mass, in which drama and revelation are joined, we find in the liturgy of Holy Week texts which run from the creation (Genesis 1 in the Easter Eve service) to man's redemption: a microcosm of the total world order is created. Mallarmé's soteriological preoccupations are evident from an early point on, which allows us some intuition of the content of the Book, and Mallarmé's allusions to it give one to understand that it constitutes a sacred performance. Especially in the years preceding the autobiographical letter do we find references to Mallarmé's great work (II, 248, 273, 301). The remaining notes for it seem to involve a sacred book with pages to be rearranged in permutations, which would be read aloud in a ceremony; the connection with Mallarmé's theory of drama as ritual is clear. This Book was in a sense a dream of structure, a form that would represent totality. Mallarmé speaks of the poem which "ne remplace tout que faute de tout" (335), that is, substitutes itself for the unstable cycle of Being and Nothingness of which our world is made. Such a book is ideal in the special sense Mallarmé sometimes gives to the word.

"Idealism" is a term often used in connection with Mallarmé, but some discriminations are necessary to determine the meaning of it most appropriate in speaking of him. This meaning is not at all the one applicable to minor Symbolist writings. When Jean Moréas, in the Manifeste du Symbolisme, or André Gide, in the Traité du Narcisse, refer to the Idea, they allude to an abstract, more or less Platonic entity anterior and superior to things. Their Idea or Ideas can be suggested in an elaborate poetic style, if not totally captured in it. This rather literary sort of philosophy seems a trifle unserious in its solemn dualism. For Mallarmé, on the other hand, the Idea and Idealism are more nearly identifiable with the constructs of Hegelian thought, in which the Idea lies at the end of a dialectic process where both the material and the abstract play a part. Language is the place where the synthesis takes place, for it is the highest spiritual reality and not the reflection of some Platonic world of forms. It is in this sense that we must read Mallarmé's famous remarks on poetic language and the Idea which is a constituent of the total Idea:

> I say: a flower! and out of the oblivion to which my voice consigns the memory of any real forms there arises, musically, something other than the blossoms I know— the flower absent from all bouquets, the very idea in all its delicacy. (368)

We must be careful not to attribute some kind of Platonism to Mallarmé: this idea exists only in language and not at all as some heavenly archetype beyond human ken. Moreover, there is always some "reminiscence of the object" (368) in language, for the word or idea is at the end, not the beginning of the dialectic process. The world of Being and Nothingness exists at a stage of thought anterior to the discovery of the ideal realm of words. Suggestion, evocation, and allusion are terms Mallarmé used to define the relation between language and the object (366). Rather than representing, poetry has the quality of virtuality (368), a power contained within it, for it releases the idea of a word. Furthermore, the language of poetry makes up for the defects of real language, where sounds do not always suggest the thing. A verse is a new unit of expression, eliminating chance in the form of accidental associations of the individual words which compose it (368). When Mallarmé speaks of the "attempt near to creation" in language (400), he alludes to the peculiar mode of poetry by which something of mimesis remains in it, while clearly the empirical world offers nothing resembling what we perceive in it. Practical language, the reportage of the novel (368), merely represents an initial, gross kind of usage, like the logic of common sense, the empirical reason which tells us that Being and Nothingness cannot be reconciled. Mallarmé's word for moving *beyond* ordinary language is "*trans*position" (366); when linguistic relationships become complex and words modify each other in a "distant reciprocity of reflections" (386), we find outselves in a spiritual reality, a living world of discourse.

It is evident from the notions of virtuality and reminiscence of the object and of the reciprocal interaction of words that Mallarmé has resolved the problematic dualism of words and things by a kind of dialectic: the word in one sense remains close to the thing and in another sense exists in its own realm opposed to that of things. There is both a dichotomous relationship between words and things and a relationship of interdependence; from another point of view, the domain of language represents a synthesis beyond things. The seeming contradictions we find in Mallarmé's thought tend to suggest the kind of truth essential to Hegelianism, in which antitheses are valid, but do not indefinitely persist. The whole relation of poetic language to the empirical world must be grasped in terms of a simultaneous dichotomy and a unity achieved by "moving beyond," synthesis, or *Aufhebung.* However, we should not consider such patterns in thought as mere exercises in dialectic. but rather as the results of deep-rooted feelings.

III

The tendency to invest philosophical ideas with a highly personal emotivity is as strong in Mallarmé's late essays as it is in the letters dealing with the crisis of 1866-1868. However, a new term now enters Mallarmé's vocabulary, which is "mystery." Mystery is succinctly defined in one place as the "evolutive context of the Idea" (653), and it is evident that the word has a more complex meaning than it does in the Romantic writers who were so fond of it. The mystery-bearing evolutive context of the Idea is the manifold relationships in the totality of the universe, but conceived of in another mode than the purely intellectual. Mystery is a theological term for complex facts—such as the Incarnation, say—which can be abundantly and technically discussed, yet ultimately elude perfect understanding. The dialectic of Being and Nothingness is for Mallarmé just such a mystery, and Hegel's peculiar science of logic, which is not at all logic in the ordinary sense, can in general be conceived of as a way of organizing knowledge which goes beyond the empirical and practical reason Hegel so scorned. Mallarmé's conception of mystery can be seen as a highly original adaptation of Hegelian ideas to a point of view and emotive tonality which the philosopher did not share.

Mystery is common to music and poetry, according to "La Musique et les lettres." For the former, we have Schönberg's interesting suggestion that what were traditionally classified as dissonances appear as incomprehensible or mysterious to the ear, and untraditional chord progressions have a similar effect. On the technical level, we can find several elements in Mallarmé's poetry that render the elusive relationships in the universe. The first of these is the mysterious creatures who appear in Mallarmé's later prose as well as in his verse. There is a great gaping hole in the life of humanity every evening, "the maw of the Chimera unrecognized and carefully frustrated by the social arrangement" (294). The Chimera has both its mythological, awesome sense and something of the everyday French meaning of "strange fantasy"; here it stands for the ideal, ritual theater which humanity longs for instead of the realistic fare of the late 19th-century stage. A similar sense is found in the "Monster-which-cannot-be" (541), which Wagner wounds with his contemplative gaze. The notion that something exists but not quite, or exists as mere virtuality, is expressed by the definition of Hamlet as the "latent lord who cannot become" (300). Hamlet is the great example of tragedy, in which there is an antagonism between dream, in the ideal sense, and the fatalities visited upon man. The bird which folds its dying wing at dark in "Quand l'ombre menaça" symbolizes the tragic situation. Finally, Hérodiade's mode of being participates in the same kind of ontological mystery.

In all these phrases we perceive the anguish of Being and Nothingness striving to rise to the salvation of the Idea. Dialectic has intense dramatic power in Mallarmé, and nowhere do we see this better than in the second sonnet of the triptych, one of the most characteristic of Mallarmé's late pieces:

> Je crois bien que deux bouches n'ont
> Bu, ni son amant ni ma mère,
> Jamais à la même Chimère,
> Moi, sylphe de ce froid plafond!

(I, the sylph painted on this cold ceiling, am sure neither my mother nor her lover ever drank from the same dream.)

After the dying light of the first sonnet, in which the monstrous clawed feet of a console's legs grasp in agony the marble top, the room is in total darkness. The struggle for Being is over. The sylph painted on the ceiling or carved near it senses his vacuity, for the movement from the first to the second sonnet is that from Being into Nothingness. The intensity with which Mallarmé learned to render Nothingness in his late style ("Aboli bibelot d'inanité sonore") is one of his most astonishing technical feats: the concept is perceptible in all its vastness. The experience recorded in the midnight of *Igitur* returns with the exquisite stylistic deftness in which all the words of the sentence together form one great perfect vocable:

> Le pur vase d'aucun breuvage
> Que l'inexhaustible veuvage
> Agonise mais ne consent,
>
> Naïf baiser des plus funèbres!
> A rien expirer annonçant
> Une rose dans les ténèbres.

(The vase empty of any liquid other than endless widowhood is dying, but will not consent even to suggest anything so much as a rose in the darkness, like some naïve kiss of the moribund.)

"Pure" is a key word, as in *Igitur,* mysteriously negative and yet positive at once. The in-between state of what is vanishing into Nothingness is epitomized by the words *agonie* and *agoniser* indicating death-throes. Comparable passages are to be found in "Ses purs ongles" ("un or agonise"), in the "monstre d'or" alluding to death in "Toast funèbre," and, finally, in a prose passage from "La Musique et les lettres": "the death-throes convulsing the Chimera, who pours out of his golden wounds the evidence that all Being is similarly ebbing away" (648).

The mystery of Being and Nothingness is, of course, inseparable in Mallarmé's philosophical poems from soteriology, for the latter is the key to the unity of art, religion and philosophy. As Hegel put it:

> The three forms of the absolute spirit—art, religion, philosophy—represent the same Absolute. They differ only in the medium of expression. All three are ways of salvation from the oppressive and restricting problems of external nature and finite mind. (p. 285)

But the absolute is not an initial *donnée.* There is a striving towards it from Being and Nothingness, and Mallarmé's poetic language is particularly rich in articulations marking the process. The tercets of "Ses purs ongles," for example, begin "But near the window open onto the north," and the image of dying light ("un or agonise") follows; the "incomprehensible" starlight is introduced by the articulatory twist of "although . . . in the frame, soon are fixed the seven sparkling stars of the Dipper." A "but . . . although" is Mallarmé's stylistic rendering of the "relationships of all." In "Quand l'ombre menaça" a negative sentence is followed by the "yes" which introduces the final image of light. The adverbial clause most characteristic of Mallarmé's late poetry is the *if* clause, as in the first sonnet of the triptych:

> Tout Orgueil fume-t-il du soir,
> Torche dans un branle étouffée
> Sans que l'immortelle bouffée
> Ne puisse à l'abandon surseoir!
>
> La chambre ancienne de l'hoir
> De maint riche mais chu trophée
> Ne serait pas même chauffée
> S'il survenait par le couloir.

(All family pride is glorious as a sunset! and, extinguished as one shakes and smothers a torch, it gives off an immortal puff of smoke, which, however, cannot survive neglect. If the heir of many a rich trophy, fallen from the walls, came back through the hallway into his room, he would not find it even heated.)

The *sans que* provides an initial relationship and a paradoxical one. The conditional sentence further complicates the relationships with its hypothesis, and the intricate word order of the tercets holds everything in syntactical suspension—while multiplying relationships—until the declarative clause of the last two lines:

> Affres du passé nécessaires
> Agrippant comme avec des serres
> Le sépulcre de désaveu,
>
> Sous un marbre lourd qu'elle isole
> Ne s'allume pas d'autre feu
> Que la fulgurante console.

(There is no light from a fire, but merely the last glint of sun on the dazzling gilt legs of the console, on which lions' claws grasp the heavy marble top, which is like the tombstone of the heir's disavowal, in this spectacle of the inevitable death-throes of the past.)

Even in poems where the final image of light is more a conceit or a complement than a philosophical statement ("La Chevelure vol," "Victorieusement fui," "M'introduire") the relational complexity of adverbial clauses persists, and, in a general fashion, all Mallarmé's late poetry shows an astonishingly large number of *if* clauses and various subjunctives. Phrases like the "relations between everything" are not simply abstractions of thought, but are realized in discourse appealing to the sense of linguistic structure.

In the late 1860s, the salvational dialectic Mallarmé worked out seemingly on the basis of Hegel did not completely cancel out his experience of Nothingness, and he was led to write "De l'oubli magique venue" and *Igitur*, works in which the Absolute is not achieved, or, achieved, appears scarcely different from Nothingness. Something comparable happens in Mallarmé's verse beginning with the third sonnet of the triptych. The morning light brings its presumed renewal of Being to the darkened room, but the major theme underlying the sonnets is that of the heir and the continuance of the race through a further birth. The latter is obviated: the light reveals "an absent bed." A "but," however, turns the theme around:

> Mais, chez qui du rêve se dore
> Tristement dort une mandore
> Au creux néant musicien
>
> Telle que vers quelque fenêtre
> Selon nul ventre que le sien,
> Filial on aurait pu naître.

(But in him whose mind is gilded by his dream, a mandolin with its hollow musical sound chamber sadly sleeps. A Mandolin such that, near some window, one could have been born a poet from its belly.)

He who glows with dream or virtuality is the tragic Hamlet figure, and the fatalities weighing on him are the burden of Being (the first sonnet) and Nothingness (the second). For the first time, Mallarmé resorts to the conditional perfect, the tense of the now irreparable, to express how the heir, rather than procreating, could have been reborn himself in art, for Mallarmé uses the Christian symbol of rebirth for the rising to the Absolute. There is a parallelism with *Igitur*: the heir is the last of his line, and on him should be incumbent some special act to give meaning to the endless cycle of birth and death his race has experienced. Stepping beyond it into the Absolute is Igitur's way, but that poem is more abstract and philosophical, whereas here the Absolute is clearly seen as art, thanks to the musical image. There is an interesting passage in the correspondence where Mallarmé describes true glory as finding oneself living in a book, as he found himself, as artist, an important figure in *A rebours* (II, 262).

All this brings us rather far from Mallarmé's early concern with Edens and the "reciprocity of proofs" exchanged by man and his "authentic terrestrial dwelling" (545). As Mallarmé pointed out, nature yielded to music in his meditations. Finally, however, he wrote two quite overtly philosophical poems in which the religious myth of Eden and the thought of art are replaced by the old image of the sea and man's life as a ship. These are "A la nue" and *Un Coup de dés*, but before looking at the former, there are some interesting relevant passages in "La Musique et les lettres" to consider.

In this subtle and important lecture, Mallarmé draws together many of his notions of the Idea as art and arrives, at a certain point, at the ambiguity adumbrated much earlier in *Igitur*: the intellectual construct of purity and Absolute may be merely nothing. We are imprisoned in the seemingly imperative formula that only what is, is. Such is the empirical reason's teaching, to which Hegel's work is a vast reply. But Mallarmé suggests we should not immediately reject the enticement of seeing a beyond or Absolute—even if it does not exist—because it is the source of our esthetic pleasure. Postulating the Absolute is the "literary mechanism" or "trick" by which one projects on the heavens what is obviously lacking here on our earth (647). In other words, the cosmic drama may not be a true ritual drama at all, but only the view we take of some chance phenomena. There is, as it were, a heavenly emptiness to be filled, and when we feel things on earth to be too dense and overwhelming, we have the right to detach them, elevate them, and make them shine (647). The universal drama written on the folio of heaven may be no more than a beneficent fiction; the principal component of the "literary machine" may be nothing whatsoever. To express this notion of an essentially alienated cosmos or "nature in its otherness," Mallarmé wrote a sonnet which is cryptic unless we view it in the perspective of "La Musique et les lettres." The quatrains elliptically present Mallarmé's tragic notion of the fatalities weighing on man despite his dreams—Man's Passion. The ancient symbol of the ship as man's life is used:

> A la nue accablante tu
> Basse de basalte et de laves
> A même les échos esclaves
> Par une trompe sans vertu
>
> Quel sépucral naufrage (tu
> Le sais, écume, mais y baves)
> Suprême une entre les épaves
> Abolit le mât dévêtu

(Under an overwhelming storm cloud, in a shoal of basalt and lava, right at the level of the enslaved waves' echo, what ghostly shipwreck, unreported by a useless horn, destroyed the stripped mast which is the last piece of wreckage to float on the tops of the waves [you know, foam, but only slaver]?)

"What shipwreck" seems to imply a cause, an agent, and the hypothetical one is alluded to in the first tercet:

> Ou cela que furibond faute
> De quelque perdition haute
> Tout l'abîme vain éployé
>
> Dans le si blanc cheveu qui traîne
> Avarement aura noyé
> Le flanc enfant d'une sirène.

(Or what appearance of shipwreck concealed the fact that, in fury, in the absence of any higher order of destruction visited on a ship, the whole empty vast abyss of waters probably drowned, as if hungry, only a child siren, in the white streak of foam remaining?)

The "perdition haute" (perdition means "shipwreck" in French as well as "perdition") is only a possibility, but it implies a hostile universal design of a kind we have not seen before in Mallarmé. The mystery of the cosmos becomes a sinister one. However, the hypothetical design may be a false notion like any notion of the Absolute, and instead we are confronted with the meaningless lashing of the waves in an alien nature, where Being and Nothingness pursue their endless cycle. The paradox of this is expressed by the impossible drowning siren, another of those creatures of half life, between Being and Nothingness, so characteristic of Mallarmé.

In "A la nue" Mallarmé employs his conception of the drama of Man's Passion played out against the "page of sky." This one and only dramatic subject received its fullest development somewhat later in Un coup de dés jamais n'abolira le hasard, where the sky and sea are again present as the background of a shipwreck, the "naufrage cela direct de l'homme." Mallarmé's idea of the great tragic conflict of dream and the fatalities inflicted upon man is brilliantly rendered in *Un Coup de dés* by the parallel, but distinct typographic and syntactic unfolding of two juxtaposed ideas. Man's aspirations are dealt with in the account of the ship's master and his son, who must cast the dice, an affirmation of the human mind.[12] In large capitals, however, the spine sentence ("A throw of dice will never abolish chance") is spread out through the first eleven of the thirteen pages of the poem: there fatality is expressed simultaneously with the story of the ship in an elaborate interplay of paradox and irony.

It is noteworthy that *Un Coup de dés* marks a retreat from the estheticizing tendencies of "Toast funèbre," "Prose pour des Esseintes," and the final sonnet of the triptych. In those poems, man is seen as artist or would-be artist, whereas in *Un Coup de dés* we find again the more general Passion of Man that Mallarmé postulated as the only subject, in his writings on drama. In this sense, *Un Coup de dés* represents the ultimate outcome of all Mallarmé's meditations on the nature of theater: the preoccupations that led to the abortive notes for *Le Livre* are here realized.

I earlier described Man's Passion as "a tragic experience followed by a psychological resurrection," and the concluding pages of *Un Coup de dés* are a tentative suggestion of some result, symbolized by a constellation, of all man's mortal coil. In the penultimate sentence, we find the same kind of hesitant expression which we encounter in the alternative questions and suppositional tense ("aura noyé") of "A la nue," or the conditional perfect at the end of the third sonnet of the triptych. The next-to-last sentence of *Un Coup de dés* runs as follows (italics mine): "Nothing *probably* has taken place *but* the place, *except perhaps* high up, where there *must be* something visible." In this twisting, indirect form of expression we recognize a link between the constellation that appears, remote and mysterious, in *Un Coup de dés* and that "incomprehensible" starlight at the end of "Ses purs ongles."

I think it would be a great mistake to assume that the appearance of the constellation in *Un Coup de dés* marks a repudiation of the starless empty world of "A la nue"; in other words, Mallarmé's themes do not form a pattern of dogmatic developments, as we might expect from an academic philosopher, but rather constitute exploratory variations on his basic metaphysical concerns. We find already in earlier poems of nocturnal light the contrast between the slow groping towards the final image of the Big Dipper in "Ses purs ongles" and the direct, strongly affirmative self-illumination of the poet in "Quand l'ombre menaça" ("Oui, je sais que . . ."). The tonal effect of *Un Coup de dés* is, however, quite new in Mallarmé's œuvre and depends on the underlying idea of the absurd. Passionately absurd affirmations go back at least to Tertullian's defense of Christianity ("Credo quia absurdum," as he is supposed to have said) and are inherent in any antithetical, paradoxical system of thought. A paralyzing, or, as he meant it, salutary form of absurdity runs throughout *Igitur.* The idea of absurdity, if not the word, is implicit in the section of "La Musique et les lettres" where cosmic structure is seen as a possibly mendacious projection from oneself. In *Un Coup de dés,* the absurd act of casting the dice is opposed to the senseless chaotic contingency of the world. Although the action is in some ways meaningless, any manifestation of will necessarily breaks the fortuitous drift of chance, and so, if insignificant from the practical, material viewpoint, the cast of the dice is valid as an affirmation in a kind of Hegelian logic of relations.

With age, Mallarmé began to conceive of an intellectual structure in which absurdity is further justified by a potential and redeeming synthesis. This synthesis is, of course, an act of the intellect ("All Thought Emits a Cast of the Dice") and has its significance in the spiritual world of discourse rather than in the pragmatic domain. Thus the pattern described by *Un Coup de dés* can scarcely be called optimistic or pessimistic in the usual senses, for it is such an elevated concept as not to be measured in terms of vulgar distinctions, valid only for everyday life. There are grandeur and folly in it, tragedy and the indirect hint of an ultimate illumination.

IV

When we attempt to draw together and summarize the major directions of Mallarmé's thought, it becomes apparent that all ulterior ramifications grow essentially out of the theory of style he early hit on. In the first place, the distinction Mallarmé made, in his explication of "L'Azur," between chance, the principle governing the diction of personal lyricism, and structure, as he conceived of it after Poe, constitutes a basic division, on which, by analogy, a view of the world can be built. Structure is impersonal, eternal, and "pure"; that is, it has an absolute rather than fortuitous existence; an act of intellect and will brings it about. When Mallarmé distinguished between the mere revelation of "temperament" in his early poems as opposed to *Hérodiade,* in which he unconsciously put all of himself, he is observing that there are two levels in the individual, one of which obeys whatever circumstances act upon it, whereas the higher level is in contact with cosmic, fixed patterns: it is the "concrete universal." We note here that Hegel may have supplied the necessary notion for this situation: in the Concept, the individual and subjective meet the impersonal and objective. From this synthesis or hinge point, the mind may move up into the realm of the Absolute. Hegel's way of collapsing oppositions which are seemingly unresolvable serves here, as elsewhere, to permit the mind fully to realize itself.

After perceiving the distinction between chance and structure, Mallarmé made a second observation on style, from which derives the notion of the Absolute or Idea. The words of a poem are not simply structured according to a discursive, thematic arrangement, but rather each word has its place in a system in which they "reflect one another," in a complex adjustment of esthetic values. Here we see "logic," in Hegel's rather special sense of an elaborate pattern of relationships which reveals the conceptual whole, the Absolute or Idea. Again, Mallarmé's meditation on the poem leads into a Hegelian sense of totality. In particular, Mallarmé's idea that *Hérodiade* was a work whose method and content were both Beauty introduces the self-reflexive movement of Hegel's Concept thinking itself.

The superimposition of Hegelian ideas on the principles Mallarmé worked out in regard to style shows a striking if often devious affinity to exist between the two independent systems of thought. We see this in particular in the way in which Hegel's notion of Being and Nothingness is adapted to Mallarmé's view of the world process as chance or contingency. In Mallarmé's original opposition between chance and structure, the former does not have any strong implication of movement. Hegel's synthesis of Being and Nothingness into Becoming is more dynamic, but it lacks the imagistic quality proper to poetry. Mallarmé identifies chance with the endless and aimless cycle of Being and Nothingness, but stresses the vanishing of phenomena into Nothingness in a way that is scarcely Hegelian. Finally, Mallarmé's use of light and dark gives an emotive tenor to the cycle, which is further made sensible by the various representations of half-life, of creatures caught in the cycle like the sylph, the golden monster, the chimera, the unicorns and sprite, the siren, and certain birds. The result of this crossing of apparently Hegelian notions and of Mallarmé's concretizing imagination is a philosophical inspiration of much greater beauty than what we find in Mallarmé's early, pre-Hegelian poems, whose thought merely follows the Romantic pattern of paradise, fall, and rebirth. However, in regard to this last term, its para-Christian derivation presages another side of Mallarmé's mature work, in which we see the fruitful coincidence Hegel intended his philosophy to have with the patterns of Western religious thought.

The Absolute includes thought, music, poetry seen as a mass-like ceremony, and nature in its great articulations. Such might be called God's Idea, and Hegel's philosophy culminates in the analogies of art, religion, and philosophy seeking the ultimate goal. Mallarmé underscores the Christian parallel in this scheme by using the pattern of Being as life, Nothingness as death, and Absolute as rebirth. His sequence places Nothingness in the midpoint, where the classic Christian paradoxes arise: salvation is in death, but salvation is life, one dies to be born, and so forth. We can consider that, somewhat in the spirit of Hegel, but certainly following the strong para-Christian tendencies in 19th-century poetic thought, Mallarmé identified the Absolute with salvation, permitting the reader to make the further parallel, which Mallarmé emphatically did not make, between the Absolute and deity. *Néant*, his word for Nothingness, is an old term for non-God in French philosophy, and the suggestion of chaos in "chance" further relates the world of blind fortuity to separation from godhead.

Mallarmé totally rejects any notion of deity in his Absolute, despite obvious analogies, but he pursued Christian parallels beyond the idea of rebirth into the domain of Christology, with rather surprising changes wrought on the central figure and action of Christianity. Christ can be seen as at once unique and exemplary: the phrase "imitation of Christ" suggests this paradox. Mallarmé chose to use the word "Passion" in his account of man's condition, and he converts the Passion of the Son of Man into the Passion of Man, *tout court*, with some traditional support for his use of the expression in the archetypality of Christ. In general, the Passion of Man involves the interplay of fatality, in the form of the cycle of Being and Nothingness, with aspirations towards the Idea, but the crux of that Passion is self-sacrifice: Saint John's yielding to death, the artist's giving up his "temperament" for a purely impersonal existence, or the crowd losing its identity in a ritual drama transcending all notion of individual life. The self-sacrifice, we should note, is form-giving: it removes the individual from the cycle of chance and provides the structure whereby man accedes to the Absolute.

The self-sacrifice I have just spoken of is an especially good example of the way esthetic, Hegelian, and para-Christian concepts overlay one another in Mallarmé's thought. In terms of poetry, self-sacrifice means the creation of a style which is governed by objective laws and does not spring from passing emotions. As a Hegelian pattern, self-sacrifice (note the reflexive so beloved of Hegel) marks the point of intersection of the subjective and objective: man becomes the concrete universal. As a Christian concept, finally, self-sacrifice signifies the death which is an awakening to the true life. This paradox, which Hegel incorporates into his special logic of reconciling opposites, is called a mystery in Christian thought.

Obviously, the esthetic, Hegelian, and para-Christian thematics appear, predominate, and vanish in the course of Mallarmé's work, according to the conception of each poem or even each part of a poem. However, all these shifting connotations are subsumed under another threefold notion, which is that of the Word, with its special metaphysical status. Mallarmé inherited the French Romantic idea of the poetic word as logos or *Verbe*, thus joining art with religion. An in many ways more searching—because more finely argued—concept is Hegel's world of living, spiritual discourse, which is the final outcome of the mind being conscious of itself. We have here an example of that coincidence Hegel found in religion, art, and philosophy; again, Hegel's thought, beyond the question of whether Mallarmé knew this or that side of it, provides a rich background of intellectual articulations against which we may profitably see Mallarmé's achievement. Of course, to call Mallarmé a Hegelian is as simplistic as to call Marx one: everyone who made significant use of Hegel could distinguish between "what is living and dead in Hegel's philosophy," as Benedetto Croce entitled the account of his own relations with Hegel. At the same time, it is deeply impressive to see how across great cultural boundaries and through the uncertainty of early translations, oral résumés, and whatever periodical material appeared, something of Hegel's intellectual vigor and peculiar vision seems to have managed to touch Mallarmé.

V

There is profit in seeing Rimbaud and Mallarmé as isolated, if anything prophetic, figures, but there are also advantages to considering them as poets deeply entwined in the intellectual life of the 19th century. Generally, the former method of study has prevailed, and the urge to see these poets as the first modernists strongly influences attitudes towards them, to the extent that literary history appears to contain a great rupture or schism on their appearance. Having exploited this vein of criticism myself, I am intensely aware of its usefulness. However, breaks in literary history are rarely absolute; further research and the readjustment of perspective it brings reveal lines of continuity which allow us to perceive the history of art forms as whole, despite shifts and innovations. For a proper examination of such matters, however, we must often go beyond the boundaries of a certain language or literature and beyond the limits of traceable influences as well. The wholeness one seeks is not that of French or German literature so much as that of Western literary traditions, and thus Novalis, Blake, or Hegel may provide one with the needed new perspective in dealing with French poets. It is as an attempt to fill the gap which often seems to exist between Rimbaud and Mallarmé and their 19th-century context that the present work was undertaken, and it is offered as a complementary view of the two poets rather than as a peremptory revision of literary history.

NOTES

Foreword

1. John Porter Houston, *The Design of Rimbaud's Poetry* (New Haven: Yale Univ. Press, 1963; rpt. Westport: Greenwood Press, 1978).

2. There are many passages about Rimbaud and Mallarmé, with explications, in *French Symbolism and the Modernist Movement: A Study of Poetic Structures* (Baton Rouge: Louisiana State Univ. Press, 1981).

3. Quoted in Clive Hart, *Structure and Motif in Finnegans Wake* (London: Faber and Faber, 1962), pp. 49-50.

Chapter I

1. See Laurence M. Porter, "Artistic Self-Consciousness in Rimbaud's Poetry," in *Pre-Text/Text/Context*, ed. Robert L. Mitchell (Columbus: Ohio State Univ. Press, 1980), pp. 159-71.

2. For the most recent and convincing study of the dating of the poems of 1870-1871, see Marcel A. Ruff, *Rimbaud* (Paris: Hatier, 1968), pp. 34-103. For the important related problem of the manuscripts and their transmission, see Pierre Petitfils, *Les Manuscrits de Rimbaud*, Etudes Rimbaldiennes, 2 (Paris: Lettres Modernes, 1970). As for my eventual quotations from Rimbaud, the reader inexpert in such matters should know that there have been a number of serious editions of part or all of Rimbaud's work, in which there are actually few cruxes of textual reading. For a long time doubtless, the standard edition will be the one I refer to, which is the *second one* (with a change of editor) in the Bibliothèque de la Pléiade: Arthur Rimbaud, *Œuvres complètes*, ed. Antoine Adam, Bibliothèque de la Pléiade (Paris: Gallimard, 1972).

3. From an allusion in "Les Poètes de sept ans," it is presumed that the knowledge of the Bible Rimbaud was later to demonstrate came from his mother's obliging him to read Scriptures. Such a practice runs counter to prevailing Catholic habits and may be explained by the fact that she meant by it to further Rimbaud's general education, in which she took much interest.

4. I have previously treated the theological preoccupations of the major French Romantic poets, especially Hugo: *The Demonic Imagination: Style and Theme in French Romantic Poetry* (Baton Rouge: Louisiana State Univ. Press, 1969); *Victor Hugo* (New York: Twayne, 1974); and "Design in *Les Contemplations*," *French Forum*, 5 (1980), 122-40.

5. For the history of this kind of thinking, see Gérard Genette, *Mimologiques: Voyage en Cratylie* (Paris: Seuil, 1976).

6. See Ernest Delahaye, *Delahaye témoin de Rimbaud*, ed. Frédéric Eigeldinger and André Gendre (Neuchâtel: A la Baconnière, 1974), pp. 39, 339, 342-43. This

edition of published and unpublished writings on Rimbaud by his friend of adolescence has been edited with the minute care and apparatus usually reserved for the works of major poets themselves.

7. Stéphane Mallarmé, *Correspondance 1862-1871* (Paris: Gallimard, 1959), p. 275n.

Chapter II

1. Jean-Louis Baudry, "Le Texte de Rimbaud," *Tel Quel*, Nos. 35-36 (Autumn 1968-Winter 1969), 45.

2. See Ernest Delahaye, *Delahaye témoin de Rimbaud*, pp. 346-47.

3. Claude-Adrien Helvétius, *De l'esprit* (Paris: Dalibon, 1827), p. 122n.

4. Quoted in Northrup Frye, *Fearful Symmetry: A Study of William Blake* (Princeton: Princeton Univ. Press, 1947), p. 21

5. See John Porter Houston, *The Design of Rimbaud's Poetry*, pp. 95-105.

6. Ernest Delahaye, *Delahaye témoin de Rimbaud*, p. 190.

7. For such aspects of the history of theater, see Marie-Françoise Christout, *Le Merveilleux et le théâtre du silence en France à partir du XVIIe siècle* (The Hague: Mouton, 1965).

8. All problems of vocabulary in Rimbaud can now be checked in William C. Carter and Robert F. Vines, *A Concordance to the "Œuvres complètes" of Arthur Rimbaud* (Athens, Ohio: Ohio Univ. Press, 1978).

9. Jeanne-Marie Bouvier de la Motte Guyon, *Poésies et cantiques spirituels*, 4 vols. (Cologne: J. de la Pierre, 1722), I, 174.

10. See Virginia A. La Charité, "Rimbaud and the Johannine Christ: Containment and Liberation," *Nineteenth-Century French Studies*, 2, Nos. 1-2 (Fall-Winter 1973-1974), 39-60.

11. For Pelagius, see Jaroslav Pelikan, *The Christian Tradition: A History of the Development of Dogma*, I: *The Emergence of the Catholic Tradition (100-600)* (Chicago: Univ. of Chicago Press, 1971), pp. 313-16. For the Eastern Church and mysticism, see Vol. 2 of the same work: *The Spirit of Eastern Christendom (600-1700)* (Chicago: Univ. of Chicago Press, 1974), pp. 46-47.

12. See the analysis in Henri Peyre, *Rimbaud vu par Verlaine* (Paris: Nizet, 1975), p. 156. This is a much subtler biographical study than most.

13. For Wordsworth's design for his last work, see M.H. Abrams, *Natural Supernaturalism: Tradition and Revolution in Romantic Literature* (New York: Norton, 1970), pp. 17-70.

Chapter III

1. For charity and the structure of *Une Saison en enfer*, see John Porter Houston, *The Design of Rimbaud's Poetry*, pp. 137-200.

2. For Henri de Saint-Simon and his followers, see Frank E. Manuel, *Prophets of Paris* (Cambridge, Mass.: Harvard Univ. Press, 1962). Other famous social theorists Rimbaud might have looked into include Louis Blanc (*Organisation du travail*), Etienne Cabet (*Voyage en Icarie, Le Vrai Christianisme*), Auguste Comte (*Système de politique positive*), Victor Considérant (*Description du Phalanstère*), Charles Fourier (*Le*

Nouveau Monde industriel et sociétaire), Félicité de Lamennais (De l'esclavage moderne), and Pierre Leroux (De l'humanité).

3. See Martin Redeker, Schleiermacher: Life and Thought, trans. John Wallhausser (Philadelphia: Fortress Press, 1973), pp. 83-84, and for the shortly following references to Schleiermacher, pp. 36-37, 54.

4. Quoted in Northrup Frye, Fearful Symmetry, p. 30. For the most substantial relevant study, see Thomas R. Frosch, The Awakening of Albion: The Renovation of the Body in the Poetry of William Blake (Ithaca: Cornell Univ. Press, 1974).

5. See, for example, Transcendence, ed. Herbert W. Richardson and Donald R. Cutler (Boston: Beacon Press, 1969).

6. Quoted in Henri Gullemin, L'Avènement de M. Thiers et réflexions sur la Commune (Paris: Gallimard, 1971), p. 218.

7. See V.P. Underwood, Rimbaud et l'Angleterre (Paris: Nizet, 1976).

8. The poem is stylistically examined in John Porter Houston, French Symbolism and the Modernist Movement, pp. 134-38.

9. Vladimir Jankélévitch, L'Ironie ou la bonne conscience, 2nd ed. (Paris: Presses Universitaires de France, 1970), p. 11.

10. Martin Redeker, Schleiermacher: Life and Thought, pp. 55-56.

11. Ibid., p. 80.

12. Quoted in Northrup Frye, Fearful Symmetry, pp. 14, 19.

Chapter IV

1. See Austin Gill, The Early Mallarmé (Oxford: Clarendon, 1979).

2. A Roman number followed by an Arabic page number refers to Stéphane Mallarmé, Correspondance, 3 vols. (Paris: Gallimard, 1959-1969).

3. Henri Mondor, Eugène Lefébure, sa vie, ses lettres à Mallarmé (Paris: Gallimard, 1951), p. 221.

4. See Stéphane Mallarmé, Les Noces d'Hérodiade, ed. Gardner Davies (Paris: Gallimard, 1959).

5. An article was proposed in Lloyd James Austin, "Mallarmé et le rêve du 'Livre,'" Mercure de France, No. 317 (January 1, 1953), 81-108.

6. Quotations from Hegel are from Georg Friedrich Hegel, Encyclopedia of Philosophy, ed. and trans. Gustav Emil Mueller (New York: Philosophical Library, 1959). Such references are indicated in the text by the abbreviation "p." before a page number.

7. Page references not preceded by a Roman numeral or by "p." are to Stéphane Mallarmé, Œuvres complètes, Bibliothèque de la Pléiade (Paris: Gallimard, 1948).

8. See Henri Mondor, Autres Précisions sur Mallarmé et inédits (Paris: Gallimard, 1961), pp. 134-35.

Chapter V

1. See Yrjö Hirn, The Sacred Shrine (Boston: Beacon Press, 1957), pp. 77-88; and O.B. Hardison, Christian Rite and Christian Drama in the Middle Ages (Baltimore: Johns Hopkins Univ. Press, 1965), pp. 34-177.

2. For the 19th-century French scholars, see Charles Magnin, *Les Origines du théâtre moderne* (Paris: Hachette, 1838), and Edélestan Duméril, *Origines latines du théatre moderne* (Paris: Franck, 1849).

3. For a criticism of drama as ritual and a bibliography, see Brian Vickers, *Towards Greek Tragedy* (London: Longman, 1973), pp. 33-43.

4. See Frederick Brown, *Theater and Revolution: The Culture of the French Stage* (New York: Viking, 1980).

5. Mallarmé mentions Cox in a letter of 1871 (II, 22). He came to know him apparently after writing his own first poetry of the solar drama, but long before publishing his translation of Cox. For the role of the solar drama in Mallarmé's poetry, see Gardner Davies, *Mallarmé et le drame solaire* (Paris: José Corti, 1959).

6. See Richard Wagner, *Wagner on Music and Drama*, ed. Albert Goldman and Evert Sprinchorn (New York: Dutton, 1964), pp. 87-91.

7. Suzanne Bernard, *Mallarmé et la musique* (Paris: Nizet, 1959), p. 75.

8. See François-Auguste Gevaert, *Histoire et théorie de la musique de l'antiquité* (Ghent: Annoot-Braeckman, 1875-1881).

9. Arnold Schönberg, *Theory of Harmony*, trans. Roy E. Carter (Berkeley: Univ. of California Press, 1978), pp. 432-33.

10. Arnold Schönberg, *Style and Idea* (New York: Philosophical Library, 1950), p. 107.

11. See Jacques Scherer, *Le "Livre" de Mallarmé*, new ed. (Paris: Gallimard, 1977).

12. For a text, translation, and detailed commentary, see John Porter Houston, *French Symbolism and the Modernest Movement*, pp. 142-47, 271-92.

FRENCH FORUM MONOGRAPHS

1. Karolyn Waterson. *Molière et l'autorité: structures sociales, structures comiques.* 1976.
2. Donna Kuizenga. *Narrative Strategies in* La Princesse de Clèves. 1976.
3. Ian J. Winter. *Montaigne's Self-Portrait and Its Influence in France, 1580-1630.* 1976.
4. Judith G. Miller. *Theater and Revolution in France since 1968.* 1977.
5. Raymond C. La Charité, ed. *O un amy! Essays on Montaigne in Honor of Donald M. Frame.* 1977.
6. Rupert T. Pickens. *The Welsh Knight: Paradoxicality in Chrétien's* Conte del Graal. 1977.
7. Carol Clark. *The Web of Metaphor: Studies in the Imagery of Montaigne's* Essais. 1978.
8. Donald Maddox. *Structure and Sacring: The Systematic Kingdom in Chrétien's* Erec et Enide. 1978.
9. Betty J. Davis. *The Storytellers in Marguerite de Navarre's* Heptaméron. 1978.
10. Laurence M. Porter. *The Renaissance of the Lyric in French Romanticism: Elegy, "Poëme" and Ode.* 1978.
11. Bruce R. Leslie. *Ronsard's Successful Epic Venture: The Epyllion.* 1979.
12. Michelle A. Freeman. *The Poetics of* Translatio Studii *and* Conjointure: *Chrétien de Troyes's* Cligés. 1979.
13. Robert T. Corum, Jr. *Other Worlds and Other Seas: Art and Vision in Saint-Amant's Nature Poetry.* 1979.
14. Marcel Muller. *Préfiguration et structure romanesque dans* A la recherche du temps perdu *(avec un inédit de Marcel Proust).* 1979.
15. Ross Chambers. *Meaning and Meaningfulness: Studies in the Analysis and Interpretation of Texts.* 1979.
16. Lois Oppenheim. *Intentionality and Intersubjectivity: A Phenomenological Study of Butor's* La Modification. 1980.
17. Matilda T. Bruckner. *Narrative Invention in Twelfth-Century French Romance: The Convention of Hospitality (1160-1200).* 1980.
18. Gérard Defaux. *Molière, ou les métamorphoses du comique: de la comédie morale au triomphe de la folie.* 1980.
19. Raymond C. La Charité. *Recreation, Reflection and Re-Creation: Perspectives on Rabelais's* Pantagruel. 1980.
20. Jules Brody. *Du style à la pensée: trois études sur les* Caractères de La Bruyère. 1980.
21. Lawrence D. Kritzman. *Destruction/Découverte: le fonctionnement de la rhétorique dans les* Essais de Montaigne. 1980.
22. Minnette Grunmann-Gaudet and Robin F. Jones, eds. *The Nature of Medieval Narrative.* 1980.
23. J.A. Hiddleston. *Essai sur Laforgue et les* Derniers Vers *suivi de Laforgue et Baudelaire.* 1980.
24. Michael S. Koppisch. *The Dissolution of Character: Changing Perspectives in La Bruyère's* Caractères. 1981.
25. Hope H. Glidden. *The Storyteller as Humanist: The* Serées of Guillaume Bouchet. 1981.
26. Mary B. McKinley. *Words in a Corner: Studies in Montaigne's Latin Quotations.* 1981.

27. Donald M. Frame and Mary B. McKinley, eds. *Columbia Montaigne Conference Papers*. 1981.
28. Jean-Pierre Dens. *L'Honnête Homme et la critique du goût: Esthétique et société au XVIIe siècle*. 1981.
29. Vivian Kogan. *The Flowers of Fiction: Time and Space in Raymond Queneau's Les Fleurs bleues*. 1982.
30. Michael Issacharoff et Jean-Claude Vilquin, éds. *Sartre et la mise en signe*. 1982.
31. James W. Mileham. *The Conspiracy Novel: Structure and Metaphor in Balzac's Comédie humaine*. 1982.
32. Andrew G. Suozzo, Jr. *The Comic Novels of Charles Sorel: A Study of Structure, Characterization and Disguise*. 1982.
33. Margaret Whitford. *Merleau-Ponty's Critique of Sartre's Philosophy*. 1982.
34. Gérard Defaux. *Le Curieux, le glorieux et la sagesse du monde dans la première moitié du XVIe siècle: L'exemple de Panurge (Ulysse, Démosthène, Empédocle)*. 1982.
35. Doranne Fenoaltea. *"Si haulte Architecture." The Design of Scève's Délie*. 1982.
36. Peter Bayley and Dorothy Gabe Coleman, eds. *The Equilibrium of Wit: Essays for Odette de Mourgues*. 1982.
37. Carol J. Murphy. *Alienation and Absence in the Novels of Marguerite Duras*. 1982.
38. Mary Ellen Birkett. *Lamartine and the Poetics of Landscape*. 1982.
39. Jules Brody. *Lectures de Montaigne*. 1982.
40. John D. Lyons. *The Listening Voice: An Essay on the Rhetoric of Saint-Amant*. 1982.
41. Edward C. Knox. *Patterns of Person: Studies in Style and Form from Corneille to Laclos*. 1983.
42. Marshall C. Olds. *Desire Seeking Expression: Mallarmé's "Prose pour des Esseintes."* 1983.
43. Ceri Crossley. *Edgar Quinet (1803-1875): A Study in Romantic Thought*. 1983.
44. Rupert T. Pickens, ed. *The Sower and His Seed: Essays on Chrétien de Troyes*. 1983.
45. Barbara C. Bowen. *Words and the Man in French Renaissance Literature*. 1983.
46. Clifton Cherpack. *Logos in Mythos. Ideas and Early French Narrative*. 1983.
47. Donald Stone, Jr. *Mellin de Saint-Gelais and Literary History*. 1983.
48. Louisa E. Jones. *Sad Clowns and Pale Pierrots: Literature and the Popular Comic Arts in 19th-Century France*. 1984.
49. JoAnn DellaNeva. *Song and Counter-Song: Scève's Délie and Petrarch's Rime*. 1983.
50. John D. Lyons and Nancy J. Vickers, eds. *The Dialectic of Discovery: Essays on the Teaching and Interpretation of Literature Presented to Lawrence E. Harvey*. 1984.
51. Warren F. Motte, Jr. *The Poetics of Experiment: A Study of the Work of Georges Perec*. 1984.
52. Jean R. Joseph. *Crébillon fils. Economie érotique et narrative*. 1984.
53. Carol A. Mossman. *The Narrative Matrix: Stendhal's Le Rouge et le Noir*. 1984.
54. Ora Avni. *Tics, tics et tics. Figures, syllogismes, récit dans Les Chants de Maldoror*. 1984.
55. Robert J. Morrissey. *La Rêverie jusqu'à Rousseau. Recherches sur un topos littéraire*. 1984.
56. Pauline M. Smith and I.D. McFarlane, eds. *Literature and the Arts in the Reign of Francis I. Essays Presented to C.A. Mayer*. 1984.
57. Jerry C. Nash, ed. *Pre-Pléiade Poetry*. 1984.

58. Jack Undank and Herbert Josephs, eds. *Diderot: Digression and Dispersion. A Bicentennial Tribute*. 1984.
59. Daniel S. Russell. *The Emblem and Device in France*. 1985.
60. Joan Dargan. *Balzac and the Drama of Perspective: The Narrator in Selected Works of* La Comédie humaine. 1985.
61. Emile J. Talbot. *Stendhal and Romantic Esthetics*. 1985.
62. Raymond C. La Charité, ed. *Rabelais's Incomparable Book. Essays on His Art*. 1986.
63. John Porter Houston. *Patterns of Thought in Rimbaud and Mallarmé*. 1986.

French Forum, Publishers, Inc.
P.O. Box 5108, Lexington, Kentucky 40505

Publishers of *French Forum*, a journal of literary criticism